Executorship accounts

Oswald Holt Caldicott

AUDIT NOTE-BOOK. Nos. I. & II., Price 6d. (net) each,

5s. per dozen. 40/- per hundred. Issued in two Series, viz. :—

No. 1—Suitable for a Monthly Audit.

No. 2—Suitable for a Quarterly or Half-yearly Audit. Name and address printed on Covers free on orders of 100 or more copies.

AUDIT NOTE-BOOK No. 3. New and Enlarged Edition.

(For Important Audits.) 100 pages. Foolscap 4to. Price 2s. per copy, 20s. per dozen, or 70s. for 50 copies, and £5 10s for 100 copies. Name and address printed on cover if 50 or more copies are ordered.

AUDITING. A Practical Manual for Auditors. Sixth Edition.

Over 900 pages. Price 21s. net. By LAWRENCE R. DICKSEE, M.Com., F.C.A.

A New and Enlarged Edition of this Standard Work has now been issued. The text has been thoroughly revised, in part re-written, and brought entirely up to date. The Work now consists of upwards 900 pages, medium 8vo, being 100 pages more than the previous Edition, of which 50 are devoted to additions to the body of the work, and 50 to Reports of Cases.

The Legal Decisions referred to in the Work are brought up to October 1904.

Special attention has been devoted in this Edition to the Accounts of Local Authorities and their Audit, Depreciation, Sinking Funds, &c.

BANKRUPTCY. Second and enlarged Edition. Price 7s. 6d,

net. By T. M. STEVENS, D.C.L., Barrister-at-Law.

A demand has arisen for a short work on the above, which, whilst treating the subject from a legal point of view, will still *be of use mainly to Chartered Accountants* and others. The general outlines of the subject, *i.e., the text of the Acts, as explained by leading cases, is what is wanted, and what this work has endeavoured to give.*

THE BANKRUPTCY TRUSTEE'S ESTATE BOOK.

Second Edition. Price 4s. net.

Compiled by LAWRENCE R. DICKSEE, M.Com., F.C.A. Author of " Auditing," &c.

This Book contains the whole of the information likely to be required by Trustees in Bankruptcy in such a form that in conjunction with the " Record Book" it provides a complete statement of all the facts relating to any particular estate, entirely doing away with the necessity for memorandum and loose sheets, which are so frequently lost.

BOOKKEEPING, ACCOUNTS, & CALCULATIONS

relating to Hire-Purchase Wagon Trade and Colliery Royalties and Wayleaves. Price 1s. 6d. net. By GEORGE JOHNSON, F.S.S., F.C.I.S., Corporate Accountant.

BOOKKEEPING FOR COMPANY SECRETARIES.

Third Edition. Price 3s. 6d. net. By LAWRENCE R. DICKSEE, M.Com., F.C.A.

This Work (which is founded upon a course of lectures delivered under the auspices of the Council of the Institute of Secretaries) deals very fully with those questions in relation to Bookkeeping, a knowledge of which is essential upon the part of every Company Secretary. It will, therefore, be found of the greatest value to all who occupy—or expect to occupy—that position, and also to all Accountant Students.

BOOKKEEPING FOR ACCOUNTANT STUDENTS.

Fourth Edition. Complete, with Index, 10s. 6d. net. By LAWRENCE R. DICKSEE, M.Com., F.C.A. (of the firm of Sellars, Dicksee & Co.)

Contains a full and complete explanation of the *Theory of Double Entry*, and is supplemented by copious *Exercises* and *Questions* that combine to make it a work of the highest educational value.

BOOKKEEPING EXERCISES for Accountant Students

Demy 8vo., about 96 pages. Price 3s. 6d. By LAWRENCE R. DICKSEE, M.Com., F.C.A., Author of " Auditing," " Bookkeeping for Accountant Students," " Bookkeeping for Company Secretaries," &c.

COMPANY-SECRETARY, THE. Fourth Edition. Price

25s. net. (Foolscap folio.) By W. H. FOX, Chartered Accountant. Containing a Full Description of the Duties of the Company-Secretary, together with an APPENDIX of FORMS and PRECEDENTS.

EXECUTORSHIP ACCOUNTS

BY

OSWALD HOLT CALDICOTT, F.C.A.

THIRD EDITION.

London :

GEE & CO., Printers and Publishers, 34 Moorgate Street, E.C

1898.

NOTE.

ON page 10 against the marginal note "Succession Duty" it is stated that, "as the freehold works are bequeathed without any directions for sale, these pass at once without any act on the part of the Executors." This is not now correct, as since the death of my Testator and the consequent succession of his nephew, the Land Transfer Act of 1897 has been passed, under which the estate in real property vests in the Executor or Administrator, and if it has been specifically devised the assent of the Executor to the devise is necessary to complete it In the meanwhile the Executor is Trustee for the Devisee. If any rents are received while the property is in the Trustee's possession it will be necessary to open Accounts with the Property, and with the Devisee, but if the assent is given immediately it will be sufficient to make a note upon the "Principal" Account of the nature of the Property, the name of the Devisee, and the date when assent was given by the Executor.

EXECUTORSHIP ACCOUNTS.

THIS little book is founded upon an address delivered to the Chartered Accountants Students' Society of London in the year 1889, which was subsequently published, and has gone through two editions.

The changes in the forms for obtaining a Grant of Probate and for payment of the death duties, which have been introduced since the passing of the Finance Acts in 1894 and 1896 have rendered some portions of the original book obsolete, and slight alterations have been necessary to make the *pro formá* Account of the Executors' dealings with the estate administered by them consistent with these forms. It is hoped that the amended account, with the accompanying explanations, may continue to serve as an useful working model for Accountant Students' and others interested in this branch of an Accountant's Work.

The form of Account which it is desirable for an Executor to adopt is equally applicable to the office of an Administrator, but for the present purpose it is better to draw the illustration from an Executor, who has definite instructions for dealing with the estate, than from an Administrator, who administers the estate according to law.

It is, therefore, assumed that the Testator, whose estate is the subject of administration, has left a will, of which the purport is given in the following abstract, which should be written for facility of reference on the face of the Draft Account.

B

Abstract of the WILL of ARTHUR BRADSHAW, Esq., late of the Atlas Works, Bermondsey, and of No. 1,001 Hampstead Road, London, N., Mechanical Engineer.

Will dated 14th October 1890.

Testator appoints Executors and Trustees—

> His brother, JAMES BRADSHAW.

> CHARLES DRURY, of Great George Street, Westminster, Consulting Engineer.

Bequeaths to ARTHUR JAMES BRADSHAW, son of brother JAMES BRADSHAW—

(a) Goodwill of business at Atlas Works.

(b) £10,000 part of capital employed therein.

(c) Freeholds, Atlas Works, Bermondsey.

Bequeaths to Wife, MARY BRADSHAW—

(a) Jewels, trinkets, wines and consumable stores.

(b) £500 within one month of death.

(c) All household furniture, and freehold dwelling-house, No. 1,001 Hampstead Road, for life or widowhood.

Gives to executors all real estate and personal estate upon trust to convert, and out of proceeds to pay—

(a) Before mentioned legacy of £500 to wife.

(b) Legacy of £100 to each executor who shall prove the will.

(c) Legacy of £500, free of duty, to the Trustees of St. Thomas's Hospital.

And to set apart :—

(d) £10,000 to be invested upon same securities as residue, and the income thereof accumulated, until EMILY, daughter of brother James, attains 21 or marries, and thereafter income of £10,000, and of all accumulations arising therefrom, to be paid to her for life, for her sole and separate use ; and after her death the legacy and income thereof to be applied in the same manner in all respects as her share of residue.

And to invest residue upon Government securities, Mortgage of freeholds and leaseholds, with not less than 60 years to run, or upon debenture, preference, or guaranteed stock of any railway company paying a dividend upon its ordinary stock, or upon municipal securities.

Income of residue to be applied in payment to widow of £1,200 per annum for her life, and balance to be divided into two equal shares, one payable to ARTHUR JAMES BRADSHAW, and so much as is required of the remaining share to be applied to the maintenance and education of EMILY BRADSHAW until she attains 21 or marries, and, thereafter, the income to be paid to her for her sole and separate use.

If EMILY BRADSHAW's share of residuary income is insufficient for her maintenance and education the executors may resort to the income arising from the legacy of £10,000.

Upon death of wife, one half share of residue shall be paid to ARTHUR JAMES absolutely, and one half share retained in trust for EMILY, so much of the income as may be required to be applied to her maintenance, and any surplus to accumulate, until she attains 21 or marries, and thereafter to pay income to her for life, and after her death in trust for all her children, if any, in equal shares, who being sons, shall attain 21, or being daughters, attain 21 or marry, with power to apply income of their presumptive shares for maintenance and education. Accruer of shares of any children who who may die under 21 and unmarried. If no children of EMILY BRADSHAW, this share to ARTHUR JAMES BRADSHAW absolutely.

The Executors may, in their absolute discretion, allow all or any part of the capital employed in the testator's business to remain for such time and at such interest as they think fit, upon ARTHUR JAMES giving a bond for repayment.

Testator died 4th August 1894.

Will proved in the Principal Registry, 14th August 1894, by JAMES BRADSHAW and CHARLES DRURY.

Estate sworn under £96,000.

It may not infrequently be desirable to obtain the advice of a solicitor to interpret some clauses in a will, but usually an accountant's knowledge is sufficient to enable him to reduce the contents so far as they affect the accounts to a few short and intelligible sentences.

It has been thought undesirable to encumber the account with any number of testamentary intricacies, as a simple statement will serve equally well to illustrate the mode of keeping Executorship Accounts.

Journal not used.

The Journal is not usually employed in Trust Accounts, as it is an advantage to have full details upon the face of each Ledger Account, and unless the entries are very numerous, it is better to make the whole in one book, which thus becomes Journal, Cash Book, and Ledger in one. If the accounts are voluminous they may be divided into parts such as "Cash Book," "Private Ledger," and "Rent and Investment Ledger." Where a Journal is used there is a tendency to exclude information from the Ledger Accounts, and the necessity for constant reference hampers an accountant when he requires to extract information, while it reduces what should be perfect simplicity to hopeless confusion when the accounts are submitted to an executor or legatee.

Where the accounts are all entered in one book, it is convenient to adopt the following order which is arranged upon something like a principle. *Arrangement of Accounts.*

First in order is an account of the Principal of the Estate, having in immediate succession the Subsidiary Accounts, such as "Funeral Expenses," "Testamentary Expenses," "Executorship Expenses," "Debts," and "Legacies," and where the estate comprises many investments a classification of them may be made for entry on the credit side of the account under their respective Subsidiary Accounts, and in the order of the Residuary Account; but it is better, as a rule, to avoid subdivision of the credits, and to make the one account a complete and continuous record of the realisation of the estate. *Principal and its Subsidiary Accounts.*

Next follows "Income," and then the "Cash Account," after which come the Personal Accounts, grouped as follows: *Income, Cash, and Personal.*

1.—Bankers.

2.—Testator's trade, shares, properties, loan and mortgages.

3.—Annuitants.

4.—Legatees.

In the *pro formâ* statement, which is appended to show the working of a set of Executorship Accounts, the entries have been restricted as far as possible to one of each kind, and with this view, in some instances, round figures have been used to complete the account where exact figures have previously been used by way of illustration.

Intention to show Duties.

Returning now to the abstract of the will, it will be seen that the testator, having no children, bequeaths the bulk of his property, subject to an annuity in favour of his widow, to a nephew and niece. The intention in having a childless testator was to admit an illustration of the payment of legacy duty, which does not arise if the bequests are to children, now that the one per cent. duty is abolished.

The next step is to see what the executors have to do, and learn from their accounts how they carry out the testator's directions.

Succession Duty.

Firstly, as the freehold works are bequeathed to the nephew without any directions for sale, these pass at once without any act upon the part of the executors ; but, as the successor is liable to pay duty, he may probably ask the accountant to prepare the necessary form, which will be found numbered 6 in the schedule.

The affidavit for probate is prepared by the solicitor, but as the accountant is often asked to furnish particulars of the estate and of the testator's debts, it is desirable to include this form properly filled up in the schedule. (*See Form A*.)

Estate Duty.

It has been necessary to provide a sum of £5,587 for estate duty and fees, and, as the executors have been satisfied that a large estate must come into their hands, they have obtained, on their own responsibility, an advance of the requisite amount from the testator's bankers ; but, as the set of accounts will clearly and fully narrate the history of the administration, it will be the best course to turn to it and let it speak for itself.

History of Administration shown by Statement of Accounts.

The executors have to account for the estate of the testator come to their hands, or to the hands of any other persons by their order, or for their use, and to show that they have dealt with the whole in due course of administration.

Commencing with the Account of Principal in the set of accounts, it will appear that the testator died on the 4th August 1894, and that he left a small sum in the house and a balance at his bankers; that he had a considerable capital in his trade, the whole of which was left by the executors in the hands of the nephew to whom the goodwill was bequeathed after obtaining valuations from properly qualified persons. The executors appear to have been justified in this course, as the amount to which he would be entitled for his legacy and share of residue would probably amount to the value left in his hands, and it was evidently the intention of the testator that he should enjoy the trade without interruption. It further appears that the goodwill of the trade, for the purpose of paying duties, was valued at £4,000, that he also possessed some railway stock and some leasehold property, and had lent £1,000 upon note of hand to a friend, and £6,000 upon mortgage.

Particulars of Estate as shown by Accounts.

In this way there is at once a record of all the property of ascertained amount, and of property which was productive at the testator's death. The cash in hand and at the bankers pass to the executors as soon as the will is proved; the capital in the trade is ascertained as quickly as possible, and brought into account; the railway stock and leasehold property are brought under notice by the proportion of the dividend and rent accrued to the death, and the loans and mortgages being ascertained amounts are at once brought into the accounts.

The properties which are not of ascertained value, and which are unproductive, do not immediately appear; but to avoid any chance of their being overlooked, an account is opened under heading which becomes a standing memorandum pending realisation.

The Principal Account will always give the property ascertained or converted, while a survey of the other accounts will give the property not converted.

The original intention was that the Principal Account should only contain property realised, and to be consistent, loans and mortgages should be excluded until they have been got in; but it will be found in practice that it saves trouble to bring them in at once, and, should there be any loss, to write that off to the debit of Principal.

Proceeding with the history of the administration, the account tells you that the executors sold the horses and carriage, and got in a life policy (an asset whose existence an accountant will always expect), and that the leasehold property was sold in June 1895. A reference to the Loan Account will tell you that it was repaid in July 1895, and a reference to the Mortgage Account will show that this was allowed to remain as an investment of the trust estate.

The will has already told you that the testator was the owner of the house in which he lived, and that he had given the use of this house and of his furniture to his wife, for her life or widowhood. You will find from this account that the wife died in January 1898, and that, shortly after her death, the house and furniture were sold and the estate divided, and that the executors retained the railway stock held by the testator as an investment of the niece's share, for which purpose it was valued at the medium price of the day.

Payments out of Principal.
The debit side of the Principal Account gives you the various classes of payments in the order of their priority, and full details of these will be found in the Subsidiary Accounts.

Under "Debts," only simple contract debts are entered, but care must always be taken, if there are other classes of debts, to enter them in the order of their priority. Care should also be taken to ascertain if rates, unpaid at the death or made afterwards, are prospective or retrospective, and to apportion them correctly between debts and payments out of income

In the "Legacies" Account some items are posted from the Personal Accounts and one from the Cash Account. The object is to facilitate reference to the will, when it is wished to ascertain if all legacies have been discharged, by showing the amount of each legacy in one sum free from any complication of duty paid in respect thereof. The precise mode in which the legacies have been discharged will be seen on reference to the Personal Accounts.

The Income Account also tells its story (which commences from the death) and shows what income was produced by the estate, and from what source income was derived and how it was applied. In this account it is desirable to give full particulars to avoid reference to the separate accounts of the properties. *Income Account.*

The Cash Account and Bank Account have no special features In the Cash Account, where the posting is to a Nominal Account, the name of the payer or payee, and the consideration should be given. *Cash Account.*

The account of the London and North Western Railway Stock has been condensed, but it will be seen that if it were made out in full, it would show that all dividends had been regularly received. *Stocks.*

Attention is called to the mode of apportionment of dividends or interest payable half-yearly, the proportion being based upon the number of days in the particular half-yearly period in which the dividend or interest arises, and not upon the number of days in a whole year. This will make a substantial difference when large sums have to be apportioned. For instance, from 1st January to 30th June comprises 181 days, whilst from 1st July to 31st December comprises 184 days, and the half-year *Apportionment of half-yearly dividends.*

from Lady-day to Michaelmas comprises 188 days, while between Michaelmas and Lady-day there are only 177 days.

Leaseholds.

The accounts of the leasehold property give particulars of the income arising therefrom, and of the ultimate realisation.

Freeholds.

The account with the freehold house, which at first is opened only as a memorandum, shows the settlement with the purchaser; certain proportions of the taxes to the date of completion being charged off to the life-tenant, and to income respectively.

Household Furniture.

The account of the household furniture is at first opened merely as a memorandum, but upon the death of the widow the realisation is here recorded.

Loan.

Henry Owen's account shows the half-yearly payments of interest, and the date of repayment of the loan.

Mortgage.

John Edward's account shows the half-yearly payments of interest, and the apportionment of interest to the date of division of the estate, when the principal sum and the interest accrued are carried forward as an investment for the niece's share.

Stock purchased by Executors.

The account following shows that on the 4th August 1895 the executors purchased Great Western Railway Debenture Stock to the value of £14,200, and that on the date of division of the estate the value had increased by £1,000, which has been carried to the credit of principal.

Legacies absolute.

The next account shows the payment of the legacy to the widow, which is made a matter of account, and then follows the annuity to the widow, which is followed by the Legacy Accounts of the executors, and the Purchase Account of the nephew, and the Residuary Legatees' Accounts of income.

Purchase of Trade Account.

From the account with Arthur James Bradshaw, Purchase of Trade Account, it will appear that acting upon the discretionary power given them by the will, the executors allowed the nephew to retain the capital in the business, after giving him credit for his legacy of £10,000, upon condition that he should pay the balance by seven yearly instalments, and should pay interest meanwhile at 5 per cent. per annum. This account further shows that the instalments and interest were regularly paid until the death of the widow, when the whole balance was discharged out of the nephew's share of *residue*. A note is made on this account, that vouchers for payment of the testator's liabilities were produced to the Executors' Accountants.

An account of money paid for maintenance of the niece is opened, and the total transferred to her Income Account upon her attaining 21, when the balance of her share of income is transferred to the account showing her share of principal, as under the will these accumulations form part of the trust funds for her benefit. *Maintenance of niece*

In compliance with the directions contained in the will, a sum of £10,000 was set apart for the testator's niece, but it was never separately invested; the executors satisfying themselves with allowing interest at 4 per cent. on the amount. This interest was added to the principal of the legacy, and the whole transferred to the account with her share of residue, when she attained 21, as there was no longer any reason for keeping the funds apart. No interest has been allowed on this sum of £10,000, until the expiration of twelve months from the death, as the bequest was not to a child of the testator. *Legacy in Trust*

The next account shows the legacy duty paid upon residue and its distribution, and particulars of this Residuary Account have been filled in upon Form No. 3. *Duty on Residue*

Each residuary legatee received a legacy of £10,000, but under the circumstances attending this administration it has not been thought necessary to deal with the duty on these sums apart from the general residue.

Shares of Residue.

Arthur James Bradshaw's share of residue is discharged by the balance due from him for purchase of the testator's trade, and by a payment in cash, and Emily Bradshaw's share together with her legacy and accumulations of income is carried forward as a trust fund to be invested for her benefit.

Income of niece's share after attaining 21.

The income arising from the investments of this trust fund will be paid over as received to the life tenant, and after her death may have to be applied for the maintenance and education of her children, with whom again separate accounts must be kept until they are respectively entitled to receive their shares.

Summary of Executors' dealings as shown by Accounts.

The executors have thus, as appears from their accounts, fulfilled all the directions of the will, down to the point of retaining the niece's share, as trustees, for herself and her children, or other successors. They have transferred the goodwill of the business to the nephew as well as his specific legacy of £10,000. They have given to the widow the jewels and household stores, and her legacy and annuity. They have after her death sold the furniture and house left for her occupation. They have paid all other legacies and can at any moment produce a clear account of their dealings with the estate.

Balance Sheet.

The Balance Sheet now stands as follows:—

	£	s	d		£	s	d
To Emily Bradshaw's share of Residue and Legacy	36,952	14	0	By Lloyd's Bank, Lim.	8,036	14	0
				,, London and North Western Railway Co., value of stock	7,600	0	0
				,, John Edwards, Principal due upon Mortgage ..	6,000	0	0
				,, Do. Interest to date	116	0	0
				,, Great Western Railway Co., value of stock	15,200	0	0
	£36,952	14	0		£36,952	14	0

The accumulations of income until the niece attained 21 were directed to be added to her share of residue, so that, so far as she is concerned, the trustees have a fresh starting point from that date; but the investments which they retain to answer her share carry a certain amount of accrued dividend or interest, which is included in the price of the day. Interest included in investments retained to answer niece's share.

It will accordingly be necessary in dealing with the income produced by these securities to pay over to the niece as income, only the balance of dividends and interest from the date of her attaining 21, to the end of the half-year, during which the dividend or interest arises. The other portions must be retained by the trustees and will be a sum for which they must find an investment. It is usual to invest as close up as possible in securities paying a fair rate of interest, and to invest the exact balance for the time being in Consols.

In the Trustee's Accounts it will be necessary to debit each investment in the income column with the balance of the half-year's dividend only, and when the cash is paid for the dividend to post the proportion accrued to the date of the niece attaining 21 in the principal column, thereby reducing the cost of the investment. For example, the further debit to the London and North Western Railway Co., at 30th June 1898 will be :

"To Emily Bradshaw, Income Account, balance of half-year's dividend, 91 days at 4 per cent, less income tax, £1 13s. 4d., £48 6s. 8d."

When the half-year's dividend, £96 13s. 4d., is received, £48 6s. 8d., only will be paid to the tenant for life and £48 6s. 8d. will remain in the trustee's hands for reinvestment as part of the principal of the Trust Fund, and the interest on the mortgage and the Great Western Railway debentures will be dealt with in like manner. Young ladies who are entirely dependent upon their income from such a trust fund are often subjected to some inconvenience at the outset, as they have no funds immediately payable to them, and only a portion of a half-year's income payable to them when the first half-year's dividends are received. The problem of how to live while the corn is growing usually has to be solved by a payment on account of income by the executor.

From this time this account will be during the niece's life a simple record of the receipt and payment of income, subject only to any changes of investment.

Upon death of niece. Upon her death accounts will have to be kept of the children's shares during infancy, or if they are all of age the fund must be got in and divided. If any reversioner has mortgaged his share and notice thereof has been given to the executor, it is a good plan to make a note of this upon the accounts.

The account, as already stated, is intended as an illustration only, and not as an exact statement, and there are details in which the working is not strictly accurate, but it will, doubtless, answer the purpose for which it is designed.

The form of account has many uses and advantages.

Advantages of this form of Executors' Accounts. *Firstly.*—It is a clear and continuous record of the executors' and trustees' dealings with the estate from the death, and the fact of such an account being kept ensures care in the administration, and is a safeguard against breaches of trust. In addition, the account is always an answer to those troublesome people who are born or married into families, and commence a disturbance because they do not find so much money as they expected, or because the trustee has offended them (very frequently by declining to commit a breach of trust).

Secondly.—The accounts are so arranged that with very little trouble the Stamp Duty Accounts can be made out from them, the order and classification of the items in the two accounts being nearly identical.

Thirdly.—If any application to the Court of Chancery be necessary in the course of the administration, the Court will often be satisfied with the production of these accounts, while, if a detailed Cash Account be required in the Chancery form, it is readily made up from the statement, and all the usual interrogatories may be readily answered.

Fourthly.—It enables the trustees to furnish the materials for a complete release, and further to bind the beneficiaries by obtaining their signatures to the detailed accounts.

Fifthly.—It ensures the receipt of all income, and its proper distribution among the persons entitled to it, and guards against any waste of principal through inadvertence.

Sixthly.—If the accounts are commenced as soon as the executors have proved the will, they ensure all these advantages at a small cost to the estate.

These advantages offer a great inducement to trustees to relieve themselves of labour and responsibility by employing an accountant. They may by doing so have a trustworthy agent who will keep the accounts, send half-yearly or other periodical statements to the beneficiaries, take proper receipts, and, in fact, manage all the current business of the trust at a cost to which no legatee can take exception.

It must not be assumed that Executorship Accounts are always capable of being dealt with as easily and clearly as those which have been put before you. Carelessness and disorder are vices to which both testators and executors are subject, and frequently an accountant is employed because no one without his special training, and the patience which it

Complicated Accounts to be unravelled.

engenders, could bring order out of the seeming chaos result-
ing from want of system in recording transactions as they
arise.   There is no case to which the telegraphic motto of our
Institute " Unravel," applies with so great force as when we
are dealing with a mass of papers accumulated by a man who
is no longer living to furnish a clue to their meaning.

Assistance to Executor.   Apart from the accounts an accountant can often render
valuable aid to an executor by his training in administrative
work.   There are often trades to be carried on, financial
arrangements to be made, and many things to be done at
the moment with a knowledge and promptitude which arises
from practice as liquidators and trustees.   But the present
subject deals only with Executorship Accounts, and a few
general hints as to the mode of dealing with a testator's
papers when they are first received, will usefully conclude
these remarks.   It may be assumed that all men, no matter
Advantage of finding idiosyncracy.   how unmethodical they may appear, have a system of dealing with papers and documents; it may be a very bad and
imperfect system, but it is there, and the accountant's first care
must be to find it out, as, once found, it will materially
assist him in understanding the testator's affairs.   Sometimes
it may not appear until weeks have been spent upon the
papers, but there is little doubt that the system is there.
Short direction as to arrange-ment of papers.   Firstly, it is desirable to run quickly through the papers,
discarding all which are manifestly irrelevant, then to
classify the remainder, and, as far as possible, arrange them
in order of date, then to proceed to reduce the information
which they contain to notes, and it will be found that by
patient comparison, an unfailing memory, and that trick
which accountants acquire of recalling a figure which they
saw an hour or a week before, it is possible eventually to
construct a coherent account.   Practice and the habit of
concentration will enable the accountant to recall two or three
amounts scattered over various papers, and mentally adapt
them to balance the sum of them which has appeared else-
where.

One word of advice is desirable in conclusion—never to put hasty work into Executors' Accounts. There are so many points to be determined as to the proper destination of each figure, and there are so many subtleties which may be easily overlooked that in this, as in so many cases, the safest motto is " *Festina lente.*"

[For use where the deceased died AFTER the 1st August 1894.]

Printed by Authority.

ESTATE DUTY.

Finance Acts 1894 and 1896
(57 & 58 Vict. c. 30, and 59 & 60
Vict. c. 28).

Form A—1. [Affidavit or Affirmation for Inland Revenue.

Name and Address of Solicitor—

    Bedford & Co., Chancery Lane, London, W.C.

This form should be used in ALL CASES where the Deceased *died after the 1st August 1894*, EXCEPT where the form B—1 or A—4 is applicable.

B—1 is for Estates not exceeding £500 *in gross* value.
A—4 is for Estates consisting *exclusively* of personal property in the United Kingdom passing under the deceased's will or intestacy.

Where "Settlement Estate Duty" on settled property is payable under the Finance Act 1894, s. 5, a separate form (C—2) is supplied for the payment thereof.

Observe.—A paper of instructions (Form A—2) for the information of the executor is issued with this form. The "Warrant" (Form 17), also issued herewith, should be filled in with a summary of the duty and interest, and be transmitted with this Affidavit and the duty.

IN THE HIGH COURT OF JUSTICE.

(ENGLAND.)

PROBATE, DIVORCE, AND ADMIRALTY DIVISION.

(PROBATE.)

THE (1) *PRINCIPAL REGISTRY.*

In the Goods of *ARTHUR BRADSHAW,* deceased.

(2) *We, James Bradshaw and Charles Drury, both of 100 Great George Street, Westminster, Consulting Engineers,* (3) make oath and say as follows :—

1. We desire to obtain a grant of (4) *Probate of the Will of the above-named Arthur Bradshaw,* of (5) *No. 1,001 Hampstead Road, London, N., Mechanical Engineer, deceased who died at 1,001 Hampstead Road, London,* on the *fourth day of August,* one thousand eight hundred and ninety-four, domiciled in (6) that part of the United Kingdom called *England.*

2. The deceased left (7) *a widow and no lawful issue surviving.*

3. The account No. 1, hereto annexed, is a true account of the particulars and value, as AT THE DATE OF THE DECEASED'S DEATH, so far as *we* have been able to ascertain the same of all the personal property of the deceased, whether in possession or reversion, within t[...]

---

(1) Insert here "Principal" or "District" as required, and in the latter case add the name of the district.

(2) Insert here the name, address, and description of each person who joins in the Affidavit or Affirmation.

(3) If affirmed, substitute "do solemnly and sincerely affirm."

(4) Insert here "Probate of the Will," or "Administration with the Will annexed of the personal estate and effects," or "Administration of the personal estate and effects," as the case may be.

(5) Insert here the address and occupation of Deceased, and his or her personal description, as "Bachelor," "Spinster," "Widower," or "Widow."

United Kingdom, (⁶) exclusive of what the deceased may have been possessed of or entitled to as a trustee and not beneficially, but including personal property over which the deceased had and exercised an absolute power of appointment. The gross value thereof, as at the date of the deceased's death, was altogether £93,952 7s. 9d., and (⁷) the whole (⁷) thereof, amounting in value to £93,952 7s. 9d., was then situate in England.

4. The first part of Schedule No. 1, hereto annexed, contains a true and particular list of the debts (⁹) due and owing from the deceased at the time of *his* death to persons resident *within the United Kingdom*, or due to persons resident out of the United Kingdom, but contracted to be paid in the United Kingdom, or charged on property situate in the United Kingdom, with the names and addresses of the several persons to whom the same are respectively due, and the descriptions and amounts of such debts. The second part of the same schedule contains a true account of the funeral expenses of the deceased.

5. The aggregate amount of the debts and funeral expenses in the said Schedule No. 1, is £15,519 11s. 9d., which, being deducted from the value of the personal property as specified in the said account No. 1, reduces such value to the sum of £78,432 16s. 0d.

8. The said debts in the said Schedule No. 1, are payable by law out of the personal property comprised in the said Account No. 1. They were incurred by the deceased *bonâ fide* for full consideration in money or money's worth wholly for the deceased's own use or benefit. They are not, nor are any of them, debts which are primarily payable out of any real property (¹¹) or debts in respect whereof there is a right to reimbursement from any other property or person (¹²).

10. There was (¹⁴) NO OTHER personal property of which the deceased was at the time of *his* death *competent to dispose*, within the meaning of the Finance Act 1894, but of which he did not dispose.

13. To the best of *our* knowledge and belief there is (¹⁷) *no* other property [UNDER ANY TITLE WHATSOEVER], beyond that already referred to, in respect of which Estate Duty is payable on the death of the deceased.

Observe.—Where the Estate Duty in respect of such other property is to be now paid, the Account No. 4 or No. 5 or the Form C—1, according to circumstances, should be used, and will be the "appropriate account." Where the duty is not to be now paid, an account in appropriate form on a separate paper should be annexed to the affidavit.

All which is true to the best of *our* knowledge and belief.

(²³) Sworn by the above-named *James Bradshaw* at *Westminster*, this *fourteenth* day of *August 1894*.

Before me, *E. F.*,
a Commissioner for Oaths.

(²⁴) Sworn by the above-named *Charles Drury* at *Westminster*, this *fourteenth* day of *August 1894*.

Before me, *E. F.*,
a Commissioner for Oaths.

(6) If deceased were domiciled abroad, insert here the name of the Country, State, Canton or Province, as the case may be, and strike out the rest of the paragraph.

(7) Adapt to suit the facts, and strike out what is not necessary.

(9) See Finance Act 1894, s. 7, sub-sections 1 and 2, as to what debts may be deducted.

(11) A mortgage debt not created by the deceased himself but charged on real property which was acquired by the deceased subject to the mortgage is primarily payable out of such real property. A mortgage debt created by the deceased himself on his real property, but which is payable by his heir or devisee under "Locke King's Act," 17 and 18 Vict. c. 113, is a debt in respect of which there is a right to reimbursement, and it must not be deducted as against the personal property.

(12) If there is a right to reimbursement but it cannot be obtained, adapt the paragraph. A debt for payment of which the deceased was surety only must not be deducted, unless the executor has already paid it.

(14) Insert "no" if the fact is so, and strike out all remainder of paragraph after "not dispose."

(17) Read the observations at foot of page 6. Insert "no" if the fact is so, and strike out all words after "Deceased." If there is other property, strike out words in square brackets.

(22) Insert here the name of each deponent, and if affirmed, substitute "affirmed" for "sworn."

ACCOUNT No. 1.

The Property situate in Scotland and Ireland respectively should be so marked. PERSONAL PROPERTY SITUATE IN THE UNITED KINGDOM. No Foreign Property should be included in this account.

	Market Price of Stocks at date of Death (*)			Gross Principal Value at Date of Death		
	£	s	d	£	s	d
Proprietary Shares or Debentures of Public Companies (A). Guaranteed 4% Stock of the London and North-Western Railway	5,000	0	0			
142				7,100	0	0
Where there is not sufficient space to insert all the particular details of the different items a separate schedule should be annexed.						
Cash in the House				20	17	6
Cash at the Bankers (B) { (1) on Drawing Account with Lloyd's Bank, Lim. .. (2) on Deposit with Lloyd's Bank, Lim. ..				1,080	12	0
Money out on Mortgage and Interest thereon to date of death, *as per statement annexed*				6,079	17	5
Money out on Bonds, Bills, Promissory Notes and other Securities, and Interest thereon to date of death, *as per statement annexed*						
Book Debts, *subject to a deduction of 5% for allowance and risks* ..				1,004	12	8
Other Debts, *as per list annexed*				38,370	0	0
Unpaid Purchase Money of Real and Leasehold Property contracted in lifetime of the deceased to be sold						
Deceased's interest in proceeds of sale of Real Property directed to be sold by settlement or by will of some other person, whether actually sold or not, estimated at (C) ..						
Personal Property over which the deceased had and exercised an absolute power of appointment (C)						
Policies of Insurance and Bonuses (if any) thereon, on the life of the deceased, viz., *Policy in the Law Life Office upon life of the deceased*				5,360	0	0
Saleable value of Policies of Insurance and Bonuses (if any) on the life of any person other than the deceased, *as per statement annexed* ..						
(D) Household Goods, Pictures, China, Linen, Apparel, Books, Plate, Jewels, Carriages, Horses, &c. *Furniture, £1,800.* If sold, realised gross £ *Jewels and Consumable Stores, £250.* (E) If unsold, estimated at £ *Carriage and Horses, £150*				2,200	0	0
				£2,200	0	0

(A) Published Quotations or Brokers' Certificates or Letters from the Secretaries of the Companies, showing the market price at the date of death, should be attached.(*)

(B) The name or names of the banks should be stated.

(C) If the power or other interest was derived under a Will, state name and date of death of the deceased, but if under a Deed, state the date, together with names and addresses of the Trustees, and if the Deed has been already produced give the official reference appearing upon it.

(D) Annex a schedule of such specific articles bequeathed for national or *quasi*-national purposes as are within the purview of sect. 15 (2) of the Finance Act 1894. See paras. 28 and 35 of Form A—2. State the value in each case, and whether the Treasury has remitted the Estate Duty thereon, and if not, whether it is intended to apply for remission. Annex also a schedule of such specific articles settled to be enjoyed in kind in succession by different persons as are within the purview of sect. 20 (1) of the Finance Act 1896. See paras. 29 and 36 of Form A—2. State the value in each case, and whether the Treasury has authorised the application of the section to them, and if not, whether it is intended to apply for authorisation. State also whether the property has yet been sold, or is in the possession of a person now competent to dispose of it.

(E) If there is a valuation, it should be annexed.

(F) State date from which profits are computed.

(G) A valuation must be annexed.

(H) These words to be cancelled where the amount is actually ascertained.

(I) No Mortgage Debt created or incurred by the deceased himself is to be deducted unless such debt was created or incurred *bona fide* for full consideration in money or money's worth wholly for the deceased's own use and benefit.

Stock in Trade. Live and Dead Farming Stock, Implements of Husbandry, &c.—
  If sold, realised gross £
  If unsold, estimated at £22,000 0 0 .... 22,000 0 0

Goodwill of business, if taken over at a price .. £
  If valued according to custom of trade .. £
  If neither, estimated at one year's profits on the average of three preceding years .. .. .. £4,000 0 0 .... 4,000 0 0
  (viz., ... years' purchase of net profits.)

(F) Profits of business from .... 189.... to date of death ...

(G) Ships and shares of Ships registered at Ports in the United Kingdom, and Profits of same to date of death, *as per statement annexed*, (H) estima ed at .. .. ..

The deceased's share in Real and Personal Property as a Partner in the Firm of *as per Balance Sheet annexed, signed by the surviving Partners* .. .. ..
  If none, estimated at .. ..

Leasehold Property (for years) *as per detailed description subjoined or annexed*—
Giving—
1. Particular description—*Four dwelling houses, Nos. 10, 11, 12, 13, New Road, Willesden.*
2. Term unexpired at date of death, *95 years*
3. Gross rents, where let, *£400 per annum,* or if not let, either the gross assessment to property tax (not the *reduced* assessment *for collection of Income Tax,* under Finance Act 1891, s. 35) or *gross* (not *rateable*) assessment to Poor Rate.
4. The Ground Rent, *£40.*
5. The nature and amount of the yearly outgoings paid by the Lessee as owner, *Repairs, £80.*

  If sold, realised gross £
  If unsold, estimated at £6,500 0 0 .... 6,500 0 0

Less (I) a Mortgage Debt of £ due from the deceased and created by an Indenture dated the _____ day of _____ 18___, for which the said Leasehold Property is the sole security.

Carried forward £93,715 19 7

---

* If business was actually done in the particular stock on the day of the deceased's death, the *average* price realised is the price to be adopted. For example:—When business was done at 98, 98$\frac{1}{16}$, and 98$\frac{3}{8}$, the market price is $\frac{98+98\frac{1}{16}+98\frac{3}{8}}{3}=98\frac{3}{16}$. If no business was done, a price one quarter up from the lower to the higher of the official "closing prices" should be adopted as an estimated price. For example:—Where the "closing prices" were "98—100," the market price is $98+\frac{100-98}{4}=98\frac{1}{2}$. Where the day of the deceased's death was a Sunday, or other day for which no prices are available, the price for the day before should be taken.

(**K**) If the life interest was derived under a will, state name and date of death of the deceased; but if under a Deed state the date, together with names and addresses of the Trustees, and if the Deed has been already produced give the official reference appearing upon it.

(**L**) All Interests in Expectancy, whether vested or contingent, should be included, whether or no the property is chargeable with Estate Duty, on the deceased's death as passing under the earlier disposition.

(**M**) But where the deceased was entitled to the interest expectant upon his own death or upon the death of another person who survives him, and Estate Duty is payable upon the corpus of the property on the deceased's death, the Interest in Expectancy is not also chargeable with Estate Duty on the deceased's death as part of his free Estate. Although, as it is, in fact, part of his free Estate, its value must be looked at for the purposes of the Probate Court. The Interest in Expectancy should be brought into this Affidavit, and be taken out again in the Summary on p. 6.

(**N**) *No deduction is to be taken here unless Treasury authority has been first obtained.*

	Gross Principal Value at date of Death.		
	£	s	d
Brought forward	93,715	19	7
Rents of the deceased's own Leasehold Property due prior to the death, but not received by the deceased, (H)			
Apportionment of the rents of the deceased's Leasehold Property to date of death, (H)	193	6	8
(K) Income accrued due, but not received prior to the death, arising from Real and Personal Property of which the deceased was tenant-for-life, or for any less period, viz.:	43	1	6
Apportionment of such Income to date of death			
The deceased Interest (L) expectant upon the death of _____ now aged _____ years, under the Will of _____ or proved _____ day of _____ under a Settlement dated the 18__ , and made between (setting out the parties to the Deed) in the Property (M) set out in the statement annexed, and of which Fund the present Trustees are—			
Other Personal Property not comprised under the foregoing heads, viz.:—			
Gross Personal Property in Account No. 1 .. .. £93,952 7 9 N.B.—This is the "gross value" which is to be carried to para. 3 on page 1.			
Deduct Total of Parts 1 and 2 of Schedule No. 1 .. .. £15,519 12 9 N.B.—This is the "aggregate amount" which is to be carried to para. 5 on page 1.			
Net Personal Property in Account No. 1 .. .. £78,432 15 0 N.B.—This is the reduced "value" which is to be carried to para. 5 on page 1.			
Deduct (N) specific articles [see note (D) on page 3] whereon Estate Duty is either not payable at all, or is not now payable £			
Balance remaining .. .. £78,432 15 0 N.B.—This is the amount of "Personal Property (Account No. 1)" which is to be carried to the Summary on page 6.	£93,952	7	9

To be signed by the persons making oath or affirmation } *JAMES BRADSHAW.*
CHARLES DRURY.

SCHEDULE No. 1.

PART 1.—An Account of the debts due and owing from the deceased, to persons resident in the United Kingdom, or due to persons resident out of the United Kingdom, but contracted to be paid in the United Kingdom, or charged on property situate within the United Kingdom.

Where the debts on the deceased's personal property exceed the value thereof, and the deficiency is a proper deduction for Estate Duty purposes against the deceased's real property, deduction of such deficiency may be taken in Schedule No. 5.

Name and Address of Creditor	Description of Debt (This should include the date and short particulars of any security for the debt)	Amount		
		£	s	d
J. Veal, Butcher	Simple Contract Debt	10	12	4
S. Doughty, Baker	Do.	5	6	8
T. Patching, Tailor	Do.	25	0	0
Hampstead Overseers	Poor Rate made 1st August ..	15	0	0
Servants	Wages	10	0	0
G. Turner	Ground Rent to 24th June ..	19	6	8
	Proportion of do. to the death ..	4	6	1
	Debts owing in respect of testator's trade, as per Schedule annexed	15,400	0	0
		£15,489	11	9

NOTE.

See Finance Act 1894, s. 7, subsecs. 1 and 2, as to what debts may *not* be deducted. A statement of any debts payable by law out of the personal property in Account No. 1, but which cannot be deducted against Estate Duty, should be annexed to the Schedule by way of rider.

Where a debt is claimed to be due to the husband or wife, or any other member of the deceased's family, a full explanation should be given, and evidence of the debt should be annexed.

A mortgage debt not created by the deceased himself but charged on real property which was acquired by the deceased subject to the mortgage is primarily payable out of such real property and must not be deducted here.

A mortgage debt created by the deceased himself on his real property, but which is payable by his heir or devisee under "Locke King's Act," 17 & 18 Vict. c. 113, is a debt in respect of which reimbursement may be claimed and must not be deducted here, unless such reimbursement cannot be obtained.

A debt for payment of which the deceased was surety only must not be deducted, unless the executor has already paid it, and cannot recover it from the original debtor.

Where the debt is for "money lent" or "overdraft" to a bank, the date of the loan and the particulars of the security, if any, given, or, if none, the facts relied on, as showing that the debt is legally recoverable, should be stated.

SCHEDULE No 1.—*continued*.

PART 2.—An Account of the funeral expenses of the deceased.

	£	s	d
Undertaker's Bill	30	0	0
	£30	0	0
Total of Parts 1 and 2	£15,519	11	9

NOTE.—The cost of mourning, tombstone, or transfer of the body of deceased to any distant place of interment are not allowed to be deducted.

To be signed by the persons } making oath or affirmation }

JAMES BRADSHAW.
CHARLES DRURY.

ACCOUNT NO. 5.

An Account of Real Property passing on the deceased's death, *whereon the Estate Duty is paid on the delivery of this affidavit.*

TITLE TO PROPERTY.—Date and short material particulars of disposition, with date of, and names of, parties to any deed, and names of any testator and date of Probate of his Will. *Where the title is under the deceased's own Will or intestacy, the fact should be clearly stated.*

Real Property passing under the Will of the deceased.

Description of property, including situation, tenure, quantity, tenants' names, and nature of tenancy, and distinguishing between arable, meadow, pasture, orchards, gardens, woods, moors, commons, wastes, pleasure grounds, building land, &c.	Gross (not rateable) value for the poor rate.	Value for Property Tax. State the gross assessment (and not the *reduced assessment for collection of Income Tax* under Finance Act 1894, s. 35)	Nature of deductions from the gross annual value. Tenants' outgoings should not be deducted unless paid by owner	Amount of deductions	Net annual value	No. of Years' purchase as estimated	Estimated principal value at date of death, and gross amount realised, *if since sold*
	£ s d	£ s d		£ s d	£ s d		£ s d
Real Property, viz.:—							
Freehold Works, called Atlas Works, Bermondsey, comprising 2,400 yards of Freehold Land, with Offices, Fitting Shops, Plant and Machinery ..	1,000 0 0	1,000 0 0	*Fire Insurance* ..	20 0 0			
			Repairs ..	100 0 0	880 0 0	15	13,200 0 0
Freehold House, Hampstead Road, in occupation of the deceased ..	240 0 0	230 0 0	*Repairs* ..	50 0 0			
			Fire Insurance ..	3 0 0	177 0 0	25	4,443 15 0
			Gross value .. Deduct total of Schedule No. 5				£17,643 15 0
			Net value				£17,643 15 0

N.B.—This is the amount to be carried to Summary.

To be signed by the persons making oath or affirmation } *JAMES BRADSHAW. CHARLES DRURY.*

Observe.—As to agricultural property, see Finance Act 1894, sec. 7 (5), and 22 (1) (g), and para. 46 of Form A—2.

If the real property include unlet fishing or sporting rights, church patronage, timber, unlet building land, mines, or other property which has no annual value, or the annual value whereof is no criterion of the principal value, full details should be given. Where the property is licensed it should be expressly so stated, and the particulars of the lease or other letting should be fully set out.

Generally, as to all property, all such particulars should be furnished as are requisite to arrive at the principal value.

[Here state name and full address of the person who pays the Duty ..]	2.	3. For use at Chief Office.
1 A.G. *James Bradshaw and Charles Drury both of* *Great George Street Westminster* Comptrolled and Registered for £ " " for Accountant-General of Inland Revenue.	Received the day of 189 , the sum of Pounds, shillings and pence, for *Estate Duty* and Interest thereon. £ " " for Commissioners of Inland Revenue. This receipt does not imply that the amount of duty is not subject to rectification.	This stamp does not imply that the rate of duty is not subject to rectification.

SUMMARY OF AFFIDAVIT.

This Summary is not on oath, and, if wrong, may be amended without the Affidavit being resworn.

Table for determining rate of Estate Duty.	Net value of Property		Table for determining Amount of Estate Duty and Interest to be now Paid	
	Personal	Real		£ s d
	£ s d	£ s d		
I. Personal Property [Account No. 1] ..	78,432 16 0		A.—Estate Duty on the *adjusted* (*) net value of the Personal Property (XV.) of 6½ per cent...	£1,372 0 0
II. " " " 2] ..			*Deduct* duty payable in any British possession, to which sec. 20 of the Finance Act 1894 applies, by reason of the deceased's death in respect of property in Account No. 2, situate in such possession. (The deduction is not to exceed the amount of the Estate Duty on the property in respect of which such duty is payable.)	
III. " " " 3 (a)] ..				
IV. " " " 3 (b)] ..				
V. " " " 4] ..				
VI. Real " " 5] ..		17,643 15 0	Net duty	
VII. Total net values of Personal and Real Property, respectively, in Accounts No. 1, 2, 3 (a), 3 (b), 4 and 5 .. £	78,432 16 0	17,643 15 0		
VIII. *Deduct* value of Interests in Expectancy in Property on the *corpus* whereof Estate Duty is payable on the deceased's death under the earlier disposition, provided that the Property is itself part of the aggregated "one estate," *but not otherwise.* [See Note (M) at page 4.] Deduct no other Interests in Expectancy here			*Deduct* duty paid or payable, to which sec. 21 of the Finance Act 1896 applies, in respect of property in Accounts Nos. 4 and 5. (The deduction is not to exceed the amount of the Estate Duty on the property in respect of which such duty has been paid or is payable.)..	
IX. Total net values of Personal and Real Property, respectively, in Accounts Nos. 1, 2, 3 (a), 3 (b), 4, and 5, for determining rate of Estate Duty			Net duty ..	
X. *Add* all other *aggregable* Property [see para. 13 of Affidavit and marginal notes 17 and 18 on page 2], passing on the deceased's death in respect of which Estate Duty is not to be paid on this Affidavit				
XI. Total net values of aggregable Personal and Real Property respectively .. .. £	78,432 16 0	17,643 15 0		
XII. Carry down into "*Personal*" column from No. XI. the Total value of Real Property £	17,643 15 0		*Add* 3 per cent. per annum interest thereon, from date of death, viz., *4th August 1894,* till date of delivery of Affirmation, viz. *14th August 1894, i.e.,* —— years and *10 days.*	3 12 0
XIII. Total net value of Personal and Real Property for determining rate of Estate Duty £	96,076 11 0			
XIV. No. XIII. as adjusted [read footnote (*)] £	96,080 0 0			
XV. The appropriate rate of Estate Duty [see para. 70 of Form A—2] is 6½ per cent.			Total duty and interest (Personal Property)	£4,375 12 0

Observe.—Only *aggregable* property is to be included here. See Finance Act 1894, s. 4.

	Net value of Property				£	s	d
Table for determining Amount of Estate Duty	Personal	Real					
	£ s d	£ s d					
XVI. Values as in No. VII. above .. .. :	78,432 16 0	17,643 15 0		B.—Estate Duty on the *adjusted* (*) net value of the real property (XXIII.) at the appropriate rate (XV.) of 5½ per cent. .. .. .. :			
XVII. *Deduct* value, or a proportion thereof, of Interests in Expectancy, such as are mentioned in Note (M) on page 4, whether the Property *is* or *is not* part of the aggregated "one estate," *including* any deducted at No. VIII. above. [Read footnote (**)]				† {Whole duty : £———} {⅛th or 1/16th thereof £———}	968	0	0
XVIII. Balance .. .. :				*If the deceased has been dead more than a year* (†§§), *and the whole duty is to be now paid*—			
XIX. *Deduct* value of *other* Interests in Expectancy, in respect of which Estate Duty is payable, but is elected to be paid when the Interest falls into possession [read footnote (**)]:— Account No.———}£ " " ———}				*Add* 3 per cent. per annum interest upon the whole duty, from 12 months after death till date of delivery of Affidavit, *i.e.,* ——— years and ——— days.. .. .. .. :			
				But if only the instalments due are to be now paid—			
XX. Net values of Personal and Real Property respectively, for determining amount of Estate Duty .. .. £	78,432 16 0	17,643 15 0		*Add* 3 per cent. per annum interest upon *whose* duty, from 12 months after death till date when *last overdue* instalment was payable, *i.e.,* ——— years and ——— months .. .. :			
XXI. *Deduct* value of Annuities provided by the deceased otherwise than by his will, which are referred to in sec. 2 (1) (d) of the Finance Act 1894, provided that the value has been brought into the Account No. 4, *but not otherwise* [read footnote (§)]				*Add* 3 per cent. per annum interest upon amount of *overdue* instalments, from date when *last overdue* instalment was payable till date of delivery of Affidavit, *i.e.,* ——— days .. :			
XXII. Balance .. .. .. £	78,432 16 0	17,643 15 0		Total duty and Interest (Personal and Real Property) paid on this Affidavit	£5,283	12	0
XXIII. No. XXII., as adjusted [read footnote (*)] .. .. .. £	78,430 0 0	17,650 0 0					

* For the purpose of computing the duty, the following adjustments should be made. See para. 72 of the Form A—2:—

Where the deceased died on or after the 1st July 1896.—The net value of the property should be decreased to an even multiple of £100 [see Finance Act 1896, sec. 17], except that where the net value exceeds £100 and does not exceed £200, the Estate Duty is £1. Thus, £1,422 should be treated as £1,400. Where duty is paid in respect of real property as well as personal property, and there is an odd fraction of £100 in the respective capitals, and the two fractions together do not amount to £100, each fraction is to be disregarded. Thus, Personal £1,422 and Real £929, should be treated as Personal £1,400 and Real £900. Where, however, the two fractions together amount to or exceed £100, whichever of the two classes of property has the larger fraction of £100 should be raised to the next multiple of £100, whilst in the other class of property the fraction should be disregarded. Thus, Personal £1,482 and Real £929 should be treated as Personal £1,400 and Real £1,000.

Where the deceased died before the 1st July 1896.—The net value of the property should be increased to an even multiple of £10 [see Finance Act 1894, sec. 17]. Thus, £1,422 should be treated as £1,430. Where duty is paid in respect of real property as well as personal property, and there is an odd fraction of £10 in the respective capitals, and the two fractions together exceed £10, each class of property should be increased to the next multiple of £10. Thus, Personal £1,482 and Real £929 should be treated as Personal £1,490 and Real £930, and Personal £1,489 and Real £922 should also be treated as Personal £1,490 and Real £930. Where, however, the two fractions together do not exceed £10, whichever of the two classes of property has the larger fraction of £10 should be increased to the next multiple of £10, whilst in the other class of property the fraction should be disregarded. Thus, Personal £1,482 and Real £926, should be treated as Personal £1,480 and Real £930; whilst Personal £1,486 and Real £930 should be treated as Personal £1,490 and Real £920. Real £926, should be treated as Personal £1,480 and Real £930; whilst Personal £1,427 and Real £982 should be treated as Personal £1,400 and Real £900; and the duty and interest should be Real £1,000.

The values, so *adjusted*, should be written in the spaces provided (XXIII.) below the true values (XX. or XXII.), and the duty and interest should be computed upon the *adjusted* values and not upon the true values.

** If the property, the subject of the Interest in Expectancy, which forms an "estate by itself," is chargeable at the *same* or a *higher* rate of Estate Real property directed to be sold at or after the deceased's death, whether actually sold or not, is to be treated as *real property*.

Duty than the aggregated "one estate," deduct here the *whole* value of the Interest in Expectancy. But if the "estate by its—If" is chargeable at a *lower* rate, then deduct only so much of the value of the interest as represents that lower rate. Thus, if the "estate by itself" is chargeable at 2 per cent, and the aggregated "one estate" at 3 per cent, respectively, deduct two-thirds, and if the rates are 3 per cent, and 7 per cent, respectively, deduct three-sevenths, and so on. If payment of the duty which still remains to be paid is elected to be deferred until the interest falls in possession, then deduct the *remaining* part of the value (in the above examples, one-third and four-sevenths respectively) at No. XIX.

§ The Estate Duty on the Annuities may be paid by instalments (see para. 63 of Form A—2). Deduct the *whole value* of the Annuities here, whether the duty is or is not to be paid by instalments, and fill in a Form C—3 (in duplicate) adapting it as necessary. Annex the forms to the Affidavit, and instructions for the payment of the whole duty, or the instalment or instalments due, as may be desired, will be issued after the grant of representation has issued. No interest is chargeable for the first year after the death.

‡ If at the time of the delivery of this Affidavit *not more than* 12 months have expired since the date of the deceased's death, carry out the whole duty or ⅛th or ¼th of it, according as the duty is to be paid in one sum, or by yearly or by half-yearly instalments. No interest is chargeable.

§§ Where at the time of the delivery of this Affidavit *more than* 12 months have expired since the date of the deceased's death, the duty on the real property, whether it is to be paid in one sum or by instalments, is chargeable with interest. The interest is chargeable upon the *whole* unpaid duty, from 12 months after the deceased's death up to the date of payment of the duty or of an instalment thereof, although part only of the duty may be overdue. See sect. 6 (8) of the Finance Act 1894, and para. 62 of the Form A—2. Where the duty is elected to be paid by instalments, and payment is not made on a date when an instalment becomes payable, the interest upon the *whole* duty is to be calculated up to the date when the last overdue instalment was payable, and interest from that date is to be calculated upon the *overdue* instalments.

To be signed by the persons } JAMES BRADSHAW.
making the Affidavit .. } CHARLES DRURY.

Observe.—If there is any property other than that in the Accounts Nos. 1, 2, 3 (a), 3 (b), 4 and 5, in respect of which Estate Duty is payable on the deceased's death, it should, to the best of the executor's knowledge and belief, be specified in appropriate accounts annexed to this Affidavit. See Finance Act 1894, s. 8 (3), and paras. 1 to 32 of the Form A—2. The Accounts, No. 4 (Personal) and No. 5 (Real), printed on page 5 of this Affidavit, show the shape which the accounts should take. The names and addresses of trustees and of donees and other beneficiaries should in all cases be stated.

Form No. 17.   To be presented with Affidavit (Form A—1 or A—3) on payment of Duty.

[For Rates of Duty see p. 4 of Instructions on Form A—2, accompanying Form of Affidavit A—1 or A—3.]
     This Warrant should be filled up by the person presenting the Affidavit, and the duty must be paid at the same time.   Payment may be made at the Office of a Collector of Inland Revenue, in England, or the duty may be remitted by Cheque, drawn in favour of the Commissioners of Inland Revenue, and crossed "Bank of England," to the Accountant-General (Cashier), Inland Revenue, Somerset House, London, W.C., together with the Affidavit and this warrant.

For Deaths after 1st August 1894, and for Cases paying *ad valorem* duty.

Consecutive Number
(For use at Chief Office only.)

ESTATE DUTY (Finance Acts 1894 & 1896).

Surname of Applicant   *James Bradshaw and Charles Drury.*
Address   *100 Great George Street, Westminster.*
Date *14th* day of *August 1894.*

Collector's Office Stamp.

189—

Name and former Address of Deceased	Name	*Arthur Bradshaw,*
	Address	*1,001 Hampstead Road, London, N.*

Date of death, *4th* day of *August 1894.*

A SEPARATE WARRANT MUST BE USED FOR EACH AFFIDAVIT.

ABSTRACT OF AFFIDAVIT.

	Gross Capital £ s d	Debts and Deductions £ s d	Net Capital £ s d
PART I.—AGGREGABLE PROPERTY.			
Personal Property situate in the United Kingdom (Account and Schedule No. 1)	93,952 7 9	15,519 11 9	78,432 16 0
Personal Property situate abroad (Account and Schedule No. 2)			
Other Personal Property, viz. :—			
————————————(Account No. 3)			
————————————(Account No. 4)			
————————————(see para. 15 of Affdt.)			
Total Personality	93,952 7 9	15,519 11 9	78,432 16 0
Real Property (Account No. 5)	17,643 15 0		17,643 15 0
Other Real Property (see para. 15 of Affdt.)			
Totals £	111,596 2 9	15,519 11 9	96,076 11 0

Deduct value of Interests in Expectancy (and Property referred to in para. 15 of Affdt.) on which Duty is not paid   { Personality .. ..   Realty .. .. ..

Net Value of Aggregable Property on which Estate Duty is now to be paid   .. £96,076 11 0

DUTY PAYABLE.

Adjusted Net Capital on which duty is chargeable	Rate per	Duty £ s d
On £78,430 0s. 0d. Personality	at 5½	4,312 0 0
Deduct Allowance for Duty payable { in British Possessions, £ : : } { at Prior Death .. .. £ : : }	..	£
Add :—		
Interest at £3 per cent. per annum on duty payable from day after death to date of delivery of the Affidavit, both days inclusive, *i.e.,*——years and 10 days	..	3 12 0
Total ..	..	4,315 12 0
On Value of Realty now paid* £17,650 0s. 0d.	at 5½	968 0 0
Add :—		
Interest at £3 per cent. per annum on *whole* duty (or, if paid by instalments, on first instalment) from day after expiration of 12 months from the death to date of delivery of Affidavit, both days inclusive, *i.e.,*——years and——days	..	
Total Duty and Interest Payable on Aggregable Property (Part I.)		£
Do. do. on Non-aggregable Property (Part II. as over		£
Do. do. on this Affidavit		£ 5,283 12 0

The foregoing details have been compared with Affidavit,

——————pro Accountant.

* If only one instalment is to be paid on this Warrant the value of Realty to be carried out here should be ⅛ of the total net value.   If only one half-yearly instalment is to be paid, the value should be ¹⁄₁₆ of the total.   [For Part II. see over.]

PART II.—NON-AGGREGABLE PROPERTY.

	Gross Capital	Debts and Deductions	Net Capital	Rate per cent.	Duty	Deductions for Duty under Sec. 21, F.A., '96	Net Duty	Interest		Number of Separate Estates	Total of Duty and Interest on each Estate
								Number of days	Amount		
	£ s d	£ s d	£ s d	£	£ s d	£ s d	£ s d		£ s d		£ s d
PERSONAL PROPERTY:—											
Separate Estates, each of.. ::											
Do. do. ::											
Do. do. ::											
Do. do. ::											
REAL PROPERTY:—											
Separate Estates, each of.. ::											
Do. do. ::											
Do. do. ::											
Do. do. ::											

Total Duty and Interest on Non-Aggregable Property (as detailed above) .. £ : :

☞ *Here state Name and Address of the Person who forwards this Account.*

JAMES & SON, *Chartered Accountants, 59, Gresham Street, E.C.*

N.B.—This form is for Property chargeable under the Succession Duty Act, and should be delivered *in duplicate,* either personally, or by an Agent, at the Legacy Duty Office, Somerset House, London. If the accountable persons reside in the Country, it may be sent by post, addressed to "The Controller of Legacy and Succession Duties, Somerset House, London," when instructions will be given as to the payment of the Duty.

A separate form is supplied for Property chargeable under the Legacy Duty Acts.

No. 6.

INLAND REVENUE.

SUCCESSION DUTY ON REAL PROPERTY, which includes all Freehold, Copyhold, Customary, Leasehold, and other Hereditaments whether corporeal, or incorporeal.

REGISTER   of the Year 1894.   Folio

*Here state the Title, whether under Settlement, Will, Intestacy, or by Descent, and if under any Deed or other Document, the date thereof, and the names of the parties thereto.

†Here state whether Trustee, &c., or Successor.

An Account of the SUCCESSION IN REAL PROPERTY of *ARTHUR JAMES BRADSHAW, of Atlas Works, Bermondsey,* in the County of   upon † death of *Arthur Bradshaw,* who died on the *4th day of August, 1894, derived from Arthur Bradshaw,* the Predecessor under* *the Will of the said Arthur Bradshaw,* delivered by† *Arthur James Bradshaw, the Successor.*

DESCRIPTION OF PROPERTY.	Saleable Value.	Gross rack-rental or annual Value.
Freehold Works called "Atlas Works," Bermondsey, comprising 2,400 yards of Freehold Land, with Offices, Fitting Shops, Plant and Machinery, valued by Messrs. Thompson & Harris at	13,200 0 0	1,000 0 0
These Works were in the occupation of the Predecessor, and were rated to the poor at the annual value of		
TOTAL...... £	13,200 0 0	1,000 0 0

It should be stated whether the Property is let on Lease, and whether at rack-rent or at a ground rent, or in consideration of a premium (in which last two cases further Duty will be payable on the determination of the Lease).

If the space be not sufficient for all the Property comprised in the Succession, a Schedule should be annexed and the Totals inserted in this Account.

DEDUCTIONS.	Capital.	Annual Payments.
Necessary outgoings (in case the same are payable *by the* Owner, and *not by the Tenant*), viz. :—		
Chief or Ground-rent....................		
Land Tax Unredeemed..................		20 0 0
Fire insurance........................		100 0 0
Repairs..............................		
Annuities (if any) to which the Property is subject		
Interest of Incumbrances.................		
TOTAL....£		120 0 0

A Schedule, containing short particulars of each incumbrance and the names of the persons by whom it was created, should be annexed.

N.B.—No deduction can be made for contingent incumbrances, or for any incumbrance created by the Successor, or for the expense of collecting Rents, or for Income or Property Tax, or for any cost incurred in litigating the Title to the Property.

If the space be not sufficient for all the Deductions claimed, a Schedule should be annexed and the Totals inserted in this Account.

Total Gross Annual Value................	£	1,000 0 0
Total Annual Value of Deductions	£	126 0 0
Net Annual Value................	£	880 0 0

If it is intended to pay the whole Duty in advance, it should be so stated, in order that the Discount may be calculated.

I declare that this is a just and true Account of all the Succession in Real and Leasehold Property of Me *Arthur James Bradshaw*, upon the Death of the before-named *Arthur Bradshaw*, and that *I* was born on the 31st day of *May*, 1868, and am a son of a brother of the said *Arthur Bradshaw*, the Predecessor from whom the said Property is derived, *and I* intend to pay the whole duty in advance. Dated this 4th day of *April*, 1895.

(Here sign the Account). Arthur James Bradshaw.

D

ASSESSMENT.

The value of an Annuity of £   for a Life aged   is £   and

the Duty on this Sum at the rate of   per Cent. is assessed at £

By the Commissioners

RECEIPT FOR DUTY.

Received the   day of   18   , the Sum of

being the first Instalments of the Duty above-mentioned, with £   interest thereon.

Registered,   Comptrolled.   Pro Acct. and Comtr-Genl. of Inland Revenue.   Pro Receiver General of Inland Revenue.

N.B.—Interest at the rate of Four Pounds per Centum per Annum is payable, in all cases, from the time when each Instalment falls due. 31 & 32 Vict., cap. 124, sect. 9.

RATES OF DUTY.

Lineal Issue or Lineal Ancestor of the Predecessor... £1 per Cent.

Brothers and Sisters of the Predecessor and their Descendants .... £3 do.

Brothers and Sisters of the Father or Mother of the Predecessor and their Descendants...... £5 do.

Brother and Sisters of a Grandfather or Grandmother of the Predecessor and their Descendants ... £6 do.

Any other Person .... £10 do.

The Husband or Wife of the Predecessor is not chargeable with Duty; and a Successor, whose Husband or Wife is of nearer relationship to the Predecessor, is chargeable with Duty at the lower rate.

☞ OBSERVE:—The Duty is payable by eight equal half-yearly Instalments, the first to be paid Twelve Months after the Successor shall have been entitled in possession, and the seven following Instalments at half-yearly Intervals of Six Months each; and if there be any delay in payment, Penalties will be incurred.

ARTHUR BRADSHAW, Esq., DECEASED.

GENERAL STATEMENT

OF THE

TRUST ACCOUNTS.

1

Dr.　　　　　　　　　　PRINCIPAL IN ACCOUNT WITH THE ESTATE

OF THE LATE ARTHUR BRADSHAW, ESQ. *Cr.* ¹

	1894		fo.	£	s	d
Aug.	4	By Cash in the house at the death	20	20	17	6
	,,	By Lloyd's Bank, Ltd., Balance of Testator's account at the death	30	1,080	12	0
	,,	By Jewels, Trinkets, Wines and consumable Stores bequeathed to wife, valued for probate at £250	,,	,,	,,	,,
	,,	By Arthur James Bradshaw for the following Assets of the Testator's Trade, viz. :—				

Goodwill valued for probate at 1 year's profit on the average of 3 preceding years   4,000   0   0   52

Stock in Trade valued by Messrs. Smith and Johnson at 17,000   0   0   ,,

Loose Plant, Tools, and Fittings valued by Messrs. Smith and Johnson at 5,000   0   0   ,,

Book Debts amounting to £40,390 agreed to be taken subject to a deduction of 5 per cent. 38,370   0   0   ,,

64,370   0   0

	,,	By London and North Western Railway Co.—Proportion of ½ year's dividend from from 1st July upon £5,000 Guaranteed 4 per cent. Stock—35 days less I. T. 12s. 8d.	36	18	7	9
	,,	By Leasehold Houses, Willesden—Half year's Rents due 24th June, less I. T. £6 13s. 4d...	38	193	6	8
	,,	By Leasehold Houses, Willesden—Proportion of half year's rents from 24th June, 41 day's less I. T. £1 9s. 9d.	,,	43	1	6
	,,	By Henry Owen—Amount due upon note of hand dated 1st July 1894	41	1,000	0	0
	,,	By Henry Owen—Proportion of half year's interest upon £1,000 from 1st July. 35 days at 5 per cent. less I. T. 3s. 2d. ..	,,	4	12	8

By amount carried forward   ..   £66,730 18   1

1

Dr.   PRINCIPAL IN ACCOUNT WITH THE ESTATE

1898		fo.	£	s	d
Mar. 31	To Funeral Expenses, Transfer	5	30	0	0
,,	To Testamentary Expenses ,, ...	6	5,300	0	0
,,	To Executorship Expenses ,, ...	7	1,515	0	0
,,	To Debts ,, ...	8	15,489	11	9
,,	To Legacies ,, ...	9	25,250	0	0
,,	To Arthur James Bradshaw—One-half share				
	of Residue..	62	26,423	16	10
,,	To Emily Bradshaw — One-half share of				
	Residue	63	26,423	16	11
			£100,432	5	6

OF THE LATE ARTHUR BRADSHAW, ESQ Cr

		fo	£	s	d
1894	By amount brought forward ..		66,730	18	1
Aug 14	By John Edwards—Amount advanced upon mortgage of Freehold Land and Houses, Nos. 1,003 & 1,004 Hampstead Road, London, at 4 per cent.	42	6,000	0	0
,,	By John Edwards—Proportion of ½ year's interest on £6,000 from 1st April, 126 days at 4 per cent., less I. T. £2 15s. 1d.	,,	79	17	5
Sept. 30	By Cash—Hackney & Co., proceeds sale of brougham, carriage horses and harness, less commission, £8 10s	20	161	10	0
Dec. 31	By Cash—Proceeds of Policy No 10000 in the Law Life Office upon the life of Testator with bonus added	,,	5,360	0	0
1895					
June 24	By Leasehold Houses, Willesden—Amount produced by sale of this property by auction, per Smith and Johnson ..	38	7,000	0	0
1898					
Mar 25	By Household Furniture—Proceeds sale by auction of household furniture and effects upon the death of Mrs Bradshaw, per Smith and Johnson.. ..	40	2,000	0	0
,,	By Freehold House, 1,001 Hampstead Road —Amount produced by sale of this property by auction, per Smith and Johnson	39	4,500	0	0
31	By London and North Western Railway Co —£5,000 Consolidated Guaranteed 4 per cent Stock retained to answer Emily Bradshaw's share of residue. Value at £152, the medium price of this day	36	7,600	0	0
,,	By Great Western Railway Co.—Increase in value of £10,000 Stock from date of purchase	44	1,000	0	0
			£100,432	5	6

5

Dr. FUNERAL EXPENSES IN ACCOUNT WITH THE

		fo.	£	s	d
1894					
Aug. 30	To Cash—Reformed Funeral Co. .. .	20	20	0	0
Sept. 30	To Cash—G. Thompson, Gravestone and				
	Inscription	,,	10	0	0
			£30	0	0

6

Dr. TESTAMENTARY EXPENSES IN ACCOUNT WITH THE

					fo.	£	s	d
1894								
Aug. 14	To Cash—Bedford and Co. Estate Duty and							
	Fees	5,300	0	0				
	Settlement Estate Duty	287	0	0	20	5,587	0	0
						£5,587	0	0

7

Dr. EXECUTORSHIP EXPENSES IN ACCOUNT WITH THE

		fo.	£	s	d
1894					
Sept. 30	To Cash—Smith and Johnson, Valuation for				
1895	Probate	20	275	0	0
Mar. 31	To Cash—Bedford and Co., Bill of Costs for				
	proving the Will and for general busi-				
	ness connected with the administration				
1898	of the Estate	,,	500	0	0
Mar. 25	To Cash—Smith & Johnson, Auctioneer's				
	charges for the sale of Household				
	Furniture and effects, and of Freehold				
	and Leasehold Properties	,,	420	0	0
,,	To Cash—James & Son, Accountant's				
	Charges	,,	100	0	0
,,	To Cash—Bedford & Co., Bill of Costs for				
	drawing release and general business ..	,,	220	0	0
			£1,515	0	0

ESTATE OF THE LATE ARTHUR BRADSHAW, ESQ.   *Cr.* 5

1898		fo.	£	s	d
Mar. 31	By Principal—Transfer	1	30	0	0
			£30	0	0

ESTATE OF THE LATE ARTHUR BRADSHAW, ESQ.   *Cr* 6

1898		fo.	£	s	d
Mar. 31	By Principal—Transfer of Estate Duty and Fees	1	5,300	0	0
„	By Emily Bradshaw—Settlement Estate Duty on Legacy of £10,000, and on £28,765, her one-half share of the total Estate, less legacies, as shown by the Executor's Affidavit for Inland Revenue	63	287	0	0
			£5,587	0	0

Memorandum showing amount liable to Settlement Estate Duty:—

		£
Total Net Estate as per Affidavit,		£95,981
Less Legacies bequeathed by the Will		25,250
		70,731
Freeholds bequeathed to A. J. Bradshaw		13,200
		57,531
One-half is		28,765

ESTATE OF THE LATE ARTHUR BRADSHAW, ESQ.   *Cr.* 7

		fo.	£	s	d
	By Principal—Transfer	1	1,515	0	0
			£1,515	0	0

8
Dr.   DEBTS IN ACCOUNT WITH THE ESTATE

1894				fo.	£	s	d
Aug. 31	To Mary Bradshaw—J. Veal, Butcher	..		48	10	12	4
,,	To ,,	S. Doughty, Baker	..	,,	5	6	8
,,	To ,,	T. Patching, Tailor	..	,,	25	0	0
,,	To ,,	Hampstead Overseers' Poor Rate, made 1st August		,,	15	0	0
,,	To ,,	Servant's Wages ..		,,	10	0	0
,,	To Cash—G. Turner—½ year's Ground Rent of Leasehold Houses, Willesden, due 24th June, less I. T. 13s. 4d.			20	19	6	8
Sept. 30	To Arthur James Bradshaw—Liabilities in Testator's Trade, discharged by Arthur James Bradshaw, in the ordinary course of trade as vouched by the Executor's Accountants			52	15,400	0	0
1895							
Jan. 14	To Cash—Proportion of Half Year's Ground Rent of Leasehold Houses, Willesden, to 4th August, 41 days less I.T. 3s. ..			20	4	6	1
					£15,489	11	9

9
Dr.   LEGACIES IN ACCOUNT WITH THE ESTATE

1894		fo.	£	s	d
Aug. 4	To Emily Bradshaw—Legacy in trust ..	60	10,000	0	0
,,	To Arthur James Bradshaw—Part of Testator's Capital in his business, specifically bequeathed..	52	10,000	0	0
,,	To Arthur James Bradshaw—Goodwill of Trade valued for probate at 1 year's profits on the average of three preceding years £4,000 specifically bequeathed ..	,,	4,000	0	0
Sept. 4	To Mary Bradshaw—Pecuniary Legacy ..	48	500	0	0
1895					
Aug. 4	To James Bradshaw—Pecuniary Legacy ..	50	100	0	0
,,	To Charles Drury—Pecuniary Legacy ..	51	100	0	0
,,	To Cash—Trustees of St. Thomas's Hospital, Pecuniary Legacy	20	500	0	0
,,	To Cash—Duty on above Legacy	,,	50	0	0
			£25,250	0	0

OF THE LATE ARTHUR BRADSHAW, ESQ.   Cr. [8]

	fo.	£	s	d
By Principal—Transfer	1	15,489	11	9

| | | £15,489 | 11 | 9 |

OF THE LATE ARTHUR BRADSHAW, ESQ.   Cr. [9]

	fo.	£	s	d
By Principal—Transfer	1	25,250	0	0

| | | £25,250 | 0 | 0 |

10
Dr.   INCOME IN ACCOUNT WITH THE ESTATE

1895		fo.	£	s	d
Feb. 4	To Mary Bradshaw — Half-year's Annuity, less I. T. £20	49	580	0	0
Aug. 4	To Mary Bradshaw — Half-year's Annuity, less I. T. £20	49	580	0	0
„	To Arthur James Bradshaw—Half-share of Balance of Income	53	498	15	7
„	To Emily Bradshaw — Half-share of Balance of Income	54	498	15	6
			£2,157	11	1

1896		fo.	£	s	d
Aug. 4	To Emily Bradshaw—One year's interest from 4th August 1895, on £10,000 at 4 per cent., less I. T. £13 6s. 8d. ..	60	386	13	4
1897					
Aug. 4	To Mary Bradshaw—Annuity to date, less I. T. £80	49	2,320	0	0
1898					
Jan. 4	To Mary Bradshaw — Proportion of Half-year's Annuity to her death, 153 days less I. T., £16 13s. 4d.	„	483	6	8
Mar. 25	To Freehold House, Hampstead Road—Proportion of taxes from death of tenant for life to date allowed to purchaser	39	20	0	0
31	To Emily Bradshaw — Interest to date on £10,000 at 4 per cent., less I. T. £22 ..	60	638	0	0
„	To Arthur James Bradshaw—Half-share of Balance of Income	53	899	18	3
„	To Emily Bradshaw—Half-share of Balance of Income	54	899	18	3
			£5,647	16	6

OF THE LATE ARTHUR BRADSHAW, ESQ $Cr.$ 10

1894		fo.	£	s	d
Sept. 30	By John Edwards—Balance of half-year's interest on £6,000 from 4th August, 57 days at 4 per cent, less 1 T £1 4s 11d.	42	36	2	7
Dec. 25	By Willesden Rents—Balance of proportion of half-year's Rents, from 4th August	37	135	4	7
31	By London and North Western Railway Co. —Balance of half-year's dividend, from 4th August, 149 days, less I. T. £2 14s. 0d.	36	78	5	7
,,	By Henry Owen—Balance of half-year's interest on £1,000, from 4th August, 149 days at 5 per cent., less I. T. 13s 6d	41	19	10	8
1895					
June 24	By Willesden Rents—Balance of half-year's Rents	37	174	0	0
30	By Henry Owen—Half-year's interest on £1,000 at 5 per cent, less I T. 16s. 8d.	41	24	3	4
Aug 4	By Arthur James Bradshaw — One year's interest on £34,970 at 5 per cent., less I T £58 5s. 8d	52	1,690	4	4
			£2,157	11	1

1895		fo.	£	s	d
Dec. 31	By Great Western Railway Co — Half-year's interest on £10,000 at 4 per cent, less I. T. £6 13s. 4d.	44	~193	6	8
1896					
Aug 4	By Arthur James Bradshaw—One year's interest on £29,975 at 5 per cent., less I. T. £49 19s. 2d.	52	1,448	15	10
1897					
Aug 4	By Arthur James Bradshaw—One year's interest on £24,980 at 5 per cent., less I T. £41 12s. 8d	,,	1,207	7	4
Sept 30	By John Edwards—Interest to date, less I. T. £24	42	696	0	0
Dec 31	By London and North Western Railway Co. Dividends to date, less I T. £20 ..	36	580	0	0
,,	By Great Western Railway Co —Interest to date, less I. T £26 13s 4d.	44	773	6	8
1898					
Mar 31	By John Edwards—Half-year's interest on £6,000 at 4 per cent., less I T £4 ..	42	116	0	0
,,	By Arthur James Bradshaw—Proportion of 1 year's interest on £19,985, 239 days at 5 per cent., less I. T. £21 16s 8d ..	52	633	0	0
			£5,647	16	6

20
Dr.   EXECUTORS' CASH ACCOUNT IN ACCOUNT WITH THE

1894		fo.	£	s	d
Aug. 4	To Principal — Cash in the house at the death	1	20	17	6
14	To Lloyd's Bank Limd.	30	5,587	0	0
25	To ,, ,,	,,	100	0	0
30	To ,, ,,	,,	20	0	0
,,	To ,, ,,	,,	19	6	8
31	To Leasehold Houses, Willesden	38	193	6	8
Sept. 4	To Lloyd's Bank Limd.	30	445	1	6
30	To Principal—Hackney & Co., Proceeds of sale of Brougham, Carriage Horses and Harness, less commission £8 10s.	1	161	10	0
,,	To Lloyd's Bank Limd.	30	10	0	0
,,	To ,, ,,	,,	275	0	0
Oct. 14	To John Edwards	42	116	0	0
Dec. 31	To Henry Owen	41	24	3	4
1895					
Jan. 14	To London and North Western Railway Co.	36	96	13	4
,,	To Lloyd's Bank Limd.	30	19	6	8
,,	To Leasehold Houses, Willesden	38	193	6	8
31	To Lloyd's Bank Limd.	30	1,935	0	0
,,	To Duty on Residue—Arthur James Bradshaw	61	120	0	0
,,	To Principal—Proceeds of Policy No. 10000, in Law Life Office, upon the life of Testator, with bonus added	1	5,360	0	0
Feb. 4	To Lloyd's Bank Limd.	30	580	0	0
Mar. 31	To ,, ,,	,,	500	0	0
June 24	To ,, ,,	,,	19	6	8
,,	To Leasehold Houses, Willesden	38	193	6	8
	Forward ..		£15,989	5	8

ESTATE OF THE LATE ARTHUR BRADSHAW, ESQ   *Cr.* [20]

1894			fo	£	s	d
Aug 4	By Mary Bradshaw—Cash in the house, at the death, left in her hands		48	20	17	6
14	By Testamentary Expenses—Bedford & Co., Solicitors, Estate Duty and Fees, and Settlement Estate Duty		6	5,587	0	0
25	By Mary Bradshaw—On account		48	100	0	0
30	By Funeral Expenses — Reformed Funeral Co.		5	20	0	0
31	By Debts —G Turner—Half-year's Ground. Rent, Willesden, due 24th June ..		8	19	6	8
,,	By Lloyd's Bank Limd		30	193	6	8
Sept. 4	By Mary Bradshaw—Balance of Legacy ..		48	445	1	6
30	By Funeral Expenses — G. Thompson — Gravestone and Inscription		5	10	0	0
,,	By Executorship Expenses—Smith & John- son—Valuations		7	275	0	0
,,	By Lloyd's Bank Limd.		30	161	10	0
Oct. 14	By ,, ,, ...		,,	116	0	0
Dec 31	By ,, ,, ...		,,	24	3	4
1895						
Jan 14	By ,, ,, ...		,,	96	13	4
,,	By ,, ,, ...		,,	193	6	8
,,	By Debts—Proportion of Half-year's Ground Rent of Leasehold Houses, Willesden, to 4th August, 41 days, less I. T. 3s. .		8	4	6	1
,,	By Willesden Rents—Balance of Half-year's Ground Rent, less I. T 10s 4d ..		37	15	0	7
31	By Duty on Residue		61	1,935	0	0
,,	By Lloyd's Bank Limd		30	120	0	0
,,	By ,, ,, ...		,,	5,360	0	0
Feb. 4.	By Mary Bradshaw—Half-year's Annuity ..		49	580	0	0
Mar. 31	By Executorship Expenses—Bedford & Co.— Bill of Costs for proving the Will, and for general business		7	500	0	0
		Forward ..		£15,776	12	4

2)

| *Dr.* | EXECUTORS' CASH ACCOUNT IN ACCOUNT WITH THE |

1895		fo.	£	s	d
	Forward ..	..	15,989	5	8
June 24	To Leasehold Houses, Willesden	38	7,000	0	0
July 1	To Henry Owen	41	1,024	3	4
Aug. 4	To Arthur James Bradshaw	52	6,685	4	4
,,	To Lloyd's Bank Limd. .. ,,	30	580	0	0
,,	To ,, ...	,,	14,200	0	0
,,	To ,, ...	,,	200	0	0
,,	To ,, ...	,,	500	0	0
,,	To ,, ...	,,	50	0	0
,,	To ,, ...	,,	13	0	0
,,	To ,, ...	,,	97	0	0
,,	To ,, ...	,,	90	0	0
Sept. 4	To ,, ...	,,	498	15	7
1896					
Jan. 1	To Great Western Railway Co.	44	193	6	8
Aug. 4	To Arthur James Bradshaw	52	6,448	15	10
1897					
Aug. 4	To ,, ,, ,, ...	,,	6,202	7	4
	To Lloyd's Bank Limd.	30	2,320	0	0
,,	To John Edwards	42	696	0	0
Sept. 30					
Dec. 31	To London and North Western Railway Co.	36	580	0	0
1898					
Jan. 1	To Great Western Railway Co.	44	773	6	8
Feb. 4	To Lloyd's Bank Limd.	30	500	0	0
Mar. 31	To Household Furniture—Smith & Johnson				
	—Proceeds of sale of same	40	2,000	0	0
,,	To Freehold House, Hampstead Road ..	39	4,470	0	0
,,	To Lloyd's Bank Limd.	30	420	0	0
,,	To ,, ,, ...	,,	100	0	0
,,	To ,, ,, ...	,,	220	0	0
,,	To ,, ,, ...	,,	473	6	8
,,	To ,, ,, ...	,,	899	18	3
,,	To ,, ,, ...	,,	4,898	6	10

| | £78,117 | 17 | 2 |

Estate of the late Arthur Bradshaw, Esq   Cr. [20]

1895		fo	£	s	d
	Forward		15,776	12	4
June 24	By Willesden Rents—Half-year's Ground Rent, Willesden, less I. T 13s. 4d. ..	37	19	6	8
- ,,	By Lloyd's Bank, Limd	30	7,193	6	8
1895					
July 1	By ,, ,, ...	,,	1,024	3	4
Aug. 4	By ,, ,, ...	,,	6,685	4	4
,,	By Mary Bradshaw—Half-year's Annuity ..	49	580	0	0
,,	By Great Western Railway Co —Purchase of Stock	44	14,200	0	0
,,	By Emily Bradshaw's Maintenance Account —Per James Bradshaw..	55	200	0	0
,,	By Legacies—Trustees St. Thomas's Hospital	9	500	0	0
,,	By Legacies—Duty on above Legacy ..	,,	50	0	0
,,	By James Bradshaw—Legacy £97, and Duty £3	50	100	0	0
,,	By Charles Drury—Legacy £90, and Duty £10..	51	100	0	0
Sept 4	By Arthur James Bradshaw—Income Account	53	498	15	7
1896					
Jan 1	By Lloyd's Bank, Limd	30	193	6	8
Aug 4	By ,, ...	,,	6,443	15	10
1897					
Aug 4	By ,, ,, ...	,,	6,202	7	4
,,	By Mary Bradshaw—Annuity Account ..	49	-2,320	0	0
Sept. 30	By Lloyd's Bank, Limd.	30	696	0	0
Dec. 31	By ,, ,, ...	,,	580	0	0
1898					
Jan. 1	By ,, ,, ...	,,	773	6	8
Feb. 4	By Emily Bradshaw—Maintenance Account, per James Bradshaw	55	500	0	0
Mar 31	By Lloyd's Bank, Limd	30	2,000	0	0
,,	By ,, ,, ...	,,	4,470	0	0
,,	By Executorship Expenses—Smith & Johnson, Auctioneer's Charges	7	420	0	0
,,	By Executorship Expenses—James & Son, Accountant's Charges	,,	100	0	0
,,	By Executorship Expenses—Bedford & Co Solicitor's Costs	,,	220	0	0
,,	By Arthur James Bradshaw—Balance of Share of Income	53	899	18	3
,,	By Mary Bradshaw—Annuity Account ..	49	473	6	8
,,	By Arthur James Bradshaw—Balance of Share of Residue	62	4,898	6	10
			£78,117	17	2

E

30

Dr.   LLOYD'S BANK, LIMD., IN ACCOUNT WITH THE

1894									fo.	£	s	d
Aug. 4	To Principal Balance of Testator's Account											
	at the death	..	..	..	..			1	1,080	12	0
31	To Cash ..	..	..	..	..	..		20	193	6	8
Sept. 30	To ,, ..	..	..	..	..	..		,,	161	10	0
Oct. 14	To ,, ..	..	..	..	..	..		,,	116	0	0
Dec. 31	To ,, ..	..	..	..	..	..		,,	24	3	4
,,	To ,, ..	..	..	..	..	..		,,	5,360	0	0
1895												
Jan. 14	To ,, ..	..	..	..	..	..	..	,,	96	13	4
,,	To ,, ..	..	..	..	..	..		,,	193	6	8
31	To ,, ..	..	..	..	..	..		,,	120	0	0
June 24	To ,, ..	..	..	..	..	..		,,	7,193	6	8
July 1	To ,, ..	..	..	..	..	..		,,	1,024	3	4
Aug. 4	To ,, ..	..	..	..	..	..		,,	6,685	4	4
1896												
Jan. 1	To ,, ..	..	..	..	..	..		,,	193	6	8
Aug. 4	To ,, ..	..	..	..	..	..		,,	6,443	15	10
1897												
Aug. 4	To ,, ..	..	..	..	..	..		,,	6,202	7	4
Sept. 30	To ,, ..	..	..	..	..	..		,,	696	0	0
Dec. 31	To ,, ..	..	..	..	..	..		,,	580	0	0
1898												
Jan. 1	To ,, ..	..	..	..	..	..		,,	773	6	8
Mar. 31	To ,, ..	..	..	...	..	..		,,	2,000	0	0
,,	To ,, ..	..	.	..	..	..		,,	4,470	0	0

	£43,607	2	10

1898				
Mar. 31	To Balance brought forward ..	..	..	£8,036	14	0

ESTATE OF THE LATE ARTHUR BRADSHAW, ESQ.   *Cr.* ³⁰

								fo.	£	s	d
1894											
Aug. 14	By Cash	..	..	..	..	..	..	20	5,587	0	0
25	By	,,	..	..	..	..	..	,,	100	0	0
30	By	,,	..	..	..	..	..	,,	20	0	0
,,	By	,,	..	..	..	..	..	,,	19	6	8
Sept. 4	By	,,	..	..	..	..	..	,,	445	1	6
30	By	,,	..	..	..	..	..	,,	10	0	0
,,	By	,,	..	..	..	..	..	,,	275	0	0
1895											
Jan. 14	By	,,	..	..	..	..	..	,,	19	6	8
31	By	,,	..	..	..	..	..	,,	1,935	0	0
Feb. 4	By	,,	..	..	..	..	..	,,	580	0	0
Mar. 31	By	,,	..	..	..	..	..	,,	500	0	0
June 24	By	,,	..	..	..	..	..	,,	19	6	8
Aug. 4	By	,,	..	..	..	..	..	,,	580	0	0
,,	By	,,	..	..	..	..	..	,,	14,200	0	0
,,	By	,,	..	..	..	..	..	,,	200	0	0
,,	By	,,	..	..	..	..	..	,,	500	0	0
,,	By	,,	..	..	..	..	..	,,	50	0	0
,,	By	,,	..	..	..	..	..	,,	13	0	0
,,	By	,,	..	..	.	..	..	,,	97	0	0
,,	By	,,	..	..	..	..	..	,,	90	0	0
Sept. 4	By	,,	..	..	..	..	..	,,	498	15	7
1897											
Aug. 4	By	,,	..	..	..	..	..	,,	2,320	0	0
1898											
Feb. 4	By	,,	..	..	..	..	..	,,	500	0	0
Mar. 31	By	,,	..	..	..	..	..	,,	420	0	0
,,	By	,,	..	..	..	..	..	,,	100	0	0
,,	By	,,	..	..	..	..	..	,,	220	0	0
,,	By	,,	..	..	..	..	..	,,	473	6	8
,,	By	,,	..	..	..	..	..	,,	899	18	3
,,	By	,,	..	..	..	..	..	,,	4,898	6	10
,,	By Balance carried forward	..		..	..	..	,,		8,036	14	0

£43,607   2   10

[36]
Dr. LONDON AND NORTH-WESTERN RAILWAY COMPANY IN ACCOUNT

		fo.	Principal £ s d	Income £ s d
1894				
Aug. 4	To Principal—Proportion of half-year's dividend, from 1st July, upon £5,000 Guaranteed 4 per cent. Stock, 95 days, less I. T. 12s. 8d. ..	1		18 7 9
Dec. 31	To Income — Balance of half-year's dividend from 4th Aug. 149 days, less I. T. £2 14s...	10		78 5 7
1897				
Dec. 31	To Income—Dividends to date, less I. T. £20..	10		580 0 0
1898				
Mar. 31	To Principal — £5,000 Consolidated Guaranteed 4 per cent. Stock retained to answer Emily Bradshaw's share of residue, value at £152, the medium price of this day..	1	7,600 0 0	
			£7,600 0 0	£676 13 4
1898				
Mar. 31	To Balance brought forward ..		£7,600 0 0	

[37]
Dr. WILLESDEN RENTS IN ACCOUNT WITH THE ESTATE

		fo.	£ s d
1894			
Dec. 25	To Income—Balance of proportion of half-year's Rents from 4th August	10	135 4 7
1895			
Jan. 14	To Cash—Balance of half-year's Ground Rents from 4th August, less I. T. 10s. 4d.	20	15 0 7
June 24	To Cash—Half-year's Ground Rents, less I. T. 13s. 4d.	,,	19 6 8
,,	To Income—Balance of half-year's Rents..	10	174 0 0
			£343 11 10

WITH THE ESTATE OF THE LATE ARTHUR BRADSHAW, ESQ. *Cr.* [36]

		fo.	Principal			Income		
			£	s	d	£	s	d
1895								
Jan. 14	By Cash	.. 20				96	13	4
1897								
Dec. 31	By Cash	.. ,,				580	0	0
1898								
Mar. 31	By Balance carried forward .. ,,		7,600	0	0			
			£7,600	0	0	£676	13	4

OF THE LATE ARTHUR BRADSHAW, ESQ. *Cr.* [37]

		fo.	£	s	d
1894					
Dec. 25	By Leasehold Houses, Willesden—Balance of half-year's Rents from 4th August, less I. T. £5 3s. 7d.	38	150	5	2
1895					
June 24	By Leasehold Houses, Willesden — Half-year's Rents, less I. T. £6 13s. 4d. ..	,,	193	6	8
			£343	11	10

38
Dr.   LEASEHOLD HOUSES, NOS. 10, 11, 12 AND 13, NEW ROAD,
                                                        LATE ARTHUR

1894		fo.	£	s	d
Aug. 4	To Principal—Half-year's Rents, due 24th June, less I. T. £6 13s. 4d.	1	193	6	8
,,	To Principal — Proportion of half-year's Rents from 24th June 41 days, less I. T. £1 9s. 9d.	,,	43	1	6
Dec. 25	To Willesden Rents—Balance of half-year's Rents from 4th August, less I. T. £5 3s. 7d.	37	150	5	2
1895					
June 24	To Willesden Rents—Half-year's Rents, less I. T. £6 13s. 4d.	,,	193	6	8
,,	To Principal—Amount produced by Sale ..	1	7,000	0	0
			£7,580	0	0

39
Dr.   FREEHOLD HOUSE, NO. 1,001 HAMPSTEAD ROAD, LONDON, IN

1898		fo.	£	s	d
	Given to wife for life or widowhood—				
Mar. 25	To Principal—Amount produced by Sale of this Property by Auction, per Smith & Johnson	1	4,500	0	0
			£4,500	0	0

40
Dr.   HOUSEHOLD FURNITURE IN ACCOUNT WITH THE ESTATE

1898		fo.	£	s	d
	Given to wife for life or widowhood, valued for Probate at £1,800.				
Mar. 25	To Principal—Proceeds, Sale by Auction of Household Furniture and Effects upon the death of Mrs. Bradshaw, per Smith & Johnson	1	2,000	0	0
			£2,000	0	0

WILLESDEN, IN ACCOUNT WITH THE ESTATE OF THE BRADSHAW, ESQ. 88 *Cr.*

1894		fo.	£	s	d
Aug. 31	By Cash	20	193	6	8
1895					
Jan. 14	By Cash	,,	193	6	8
June 24	By Cash	,,	193	6	8
,,	By Cash—Amount produced by Sale of this Property by Auction, per Smith & Johnson	,,	7,000	0	0
			£7,580	0	0

ACCOUNT WITH THE ESTATE OF THE LATE ARTHUR BRADSHAW, ESQ. 89 *Cr.*

1898		fo.	£	s	d
Mar. 25	By Mrs. Mary Bradshaw — Proportion of Taxes to 4th January, the day of her death, allowed to purchaser	49	10	0	0
,,	By Income—Proportion of Taxes from death of Tenant-for-life to date allowed to purchaser	10	20	0	0
31	By Cash—Amount received from Smith & Johnson, Auctioneers	20	4,470	0	0
			£4,500	0	0

OF THE LATE ARTHUR BRADSHAW, ESQ. 40 *Cr.*

1898		fo.	£	s	d
Mar. 31	By Cash—Per Smith & Johnson, proceeds of Sale of Household Furniture and Effects upon the death of Mrs. Bradshaw	20	2,000	0	0
			£2,000	0	0

⁴¹
Dr.   HENRY OWEN IN ACCOUNT WITH THE

1894		fo.	£	s	d	£	s	d
Aug. 4	To Principal—Amount due upon note of hand dated 1st July 1894	1	1,000	0	0			
„	To Principal—Proportion of half-year's Interest on £1,000 from 1st July 35 days, at 5 per cent, less I. T. 3s. 2d...	„				4	12	8
Dec. 31	To Income — Balance of half-year's Interest on £1,000 from 4th August 149 days, at 5 per cent., less I. T. 13s. 6d.	10				19	10	8
1895 June 30	To Income—Half-year's Interest on £1,000 at 5 per cent., less I. T. 16s. 8d...	„				24	3	4
			£1,000	0	0	£48	6	8

⁴²
Dr.   JOHN EDWARDS IN ACCOUNT WITH THE ESTATE

1894		fo.	£	s	d	£	s	d
Aug. 4	To Principal—Amount advanced upon Mortgage of Freehold Land and Houses, Nos. 1,003 and 1,004 Hampstead Road, London, at 4 per cent. ..	1	6,000	0	0			
„	To Principal—Proportion of half-year's Interest on £6,000 from 1st April 126 days, at 4 per cent., less I. T. £2 15s.	„				79	17	5
Sept 30	To Income — Balance of half-year's Interest on £6,000 from 4th August 57 days, at 4 per cent., less I. T. £1 4s. 11d.	10				36	2	7
1897 Sept. 30	To Income—Interest to date, less I. T. £24	„				696	0	0
1898 Mar. 31	To Income—Half-year's Interest to date, less I. T. £4 ..	„				116	0	0
			£6,000	0	0	£928	0	0
1898			£	s	d	£	s	d
Mar. 31	To Balance brought forward, viz. :— Principal		6,000	0	0			
	Proportion of half-year's Interest to date					116	0	0

Estate of the late Arthur Bradshaw, Esq.   41
                                                                              Cr.

		fo.	£	s	d	£	s	d
1894								
Dec. 31	By Cash	20				24	3	4
1895								
July 1	By Cash—Principal and Interest	,,	1,000	0	0	24	3	4

£1,000 0 0	£48 6 8

Of the late Arthur Bradshaw, Esq.   42
                                                                              Cr.

		fo.	£	s	d	£	s	d
1894								
Oct. 14	By Cash	20				116	0	0
1897								
Sept. 30	By Cash	,,				696	0	0
	By Balance carried forward ..		6,000	0	0	116	0	0

| £6,000 0 0 | £928 0 0 |

44
Dr.   GREAT WESTERN RAILWAY COMPANY IN ACCOUNT WITH THE

			Principal			Income		
1895		fo.	£	s	d	£	s	d
Aug. 4	To Cash — Purchase of £10,000 4 per cent. Debenture Stock at £140 .. £14,000 0 0 Brokerage a n d Stamps 200 0 0	20	14,200	0	0			
Dec. 31	To Income—Half-year's Interest on £10,000 at 4 per cent., less I. T. £6 13s. 4d. ..	10				193	6	8
1897								
Dec. 31	To Income —Interest to date, less I. T. £26 13s. 4d.	10				773	6	8
1898								
Mar. 31	To Principal—Increase in value from date of purchase, viz. :— Present value at £152 .. .. £15,200 0 0 Less Cost .. 14,200 0 0	1	1,000	0	0			
			£15,200	0	0	£966 13	4	
1898			£	s	d	£	s	d
Mar. 31	To Balance brought forward ..		15,200	0	0			

48
Dr.   MARY BRADSHAW (WIDOW OF TESTATOR) IN ACCOUNT WITH

		fo.	£	s	d
1894					
Aug. 4	To Cash in the house at the death left in her hands	20	20	17	6
25	To Cash	,,	100	0	0
Sept. 4	To Cash to balance Legacy	,,	445	1	6
			£565	19	0

ESTATE OF THE LATE ARTHUR BRADSHAW, ESQ. *Cr.* 44

				Principal			Income		
				£	s	d	£	s	d
1896									
Jan. 1	By Cash	..	20				193	6	8
1898									
Jan. 1	By Cash	..	,,				773	6	8
Mar. 31	By Balance carried forward	..		15,200	0	0			
				£15,200	0	0	£966	13	4

THE ESTATE OF THE LATE ARTHUR BRADSHAW, ESQ. *Cr.* 48

1894		fo.	£	s	d
Aug. 31	By Debts—J. Veal, Butcher ..	8	10	12	4
,,	By Debts—S. Doughty, Baker	,,	5	6	8
,,	By Debts—T. Patching, Tailor	,,	25	0	0
,,	By Debts—Hampstead Overseers, Poor Rate made 1st August	,,	15	0	0
,,	By Debts—Servant's Wages ..	,,	10	0	0
Sept. 4	By Legacy, payable within one month of death	9	500	0	0
			£565	19	0

49
Dr.   MARY BRADSHAW (ANNUITY ACCOUNT) IN ACCOUNT WITH

1895			fo.	£	s	d
Feb. 4	To Cash ..	.. ..	20	580	0	0
Aug. 4	To Cash ..	.. ..	,,	580	0	0
1897						
Aug. 4	To Cash ..	.. ..	,,	2,320	0	0
1898						
Mar. 31	To Freehold House, Hampstead Road—Proportion of Taxes to 4th January allowed to purchaser		49	10	0	0
,,	To Cash paid to the Executors appointed by her will			473	6	8
				£3,963	6	8

Dr.   JAMES BRADSHAW (LEGACY ACCOUNT) IN ACCOUNT WITH

1895			fo.	£	s	d
Aug. 4	To Cash—Duty on Legacy at 3 per cent. ..		20	3	0	0
,,	To Cash—Balance of Legacy..		,,	97	0	0
				£100	0	0

51
Dr.   CHARLES DRURY (LEGACY ACCOUNT) IN ACCOUNT WITH THE

1895			fo.	£	s	d
Aug. 4	To Cash—Duty on Legacy at 10 per cent.		20	10	0	0
	To Cash—Balance of Legacy..		,,	90	0	0
				£100	0	0

THE ESTATE OF THE LATE ARTHUR BRADSHAW, ESQ.   *Cr* [49]

1895		fo.	£	s	d
Feb. 4	By Income—Half-year's Annuity, less I. T. £20	10	580	0	0
Aug. 4	By Income—Half-year's Annuity, less I. T. £20	,,	580	0	0
1897					
Aug. 4	By Income—Annuity to date, less I. T. £80..	,,	2,320	0	0
1898					
Jan. 4	By Income — Proportion of half-year's Annuity to her death, 153 days, less I. T. £16 13s. 4d...	,,	483	6	8
			£3,963	6	8

THE ESTATE OF THE LATE ARTHUR BRADSHAW, ESQ.   *Cr.* [50]

1895		fo.	£	s	d
Aug. 4	By Pecuniary Legacy	9	100	0	0
			£100	0	0

ESTATE OF THE LATE ARTHUR BRADSHAW, ESQ.   *Cr.* [51]

1895		fo.	£	s	d
Aug. 4	By Pecuniary Legacy	9	100	0	0
			£100	0	0

52

Dr.   ARTHUR JAMES BRADSHAW (PURCHASE OF
                                              ESTATE OF THE LATE

		fo.	Principal £ s d	Income £ s d
1894 Aug. 4	To Principal for the following assets of the Testator's trade, viz.:—			
	Goodwill valued for probate at 1 year's profits on the average of 3 preceding years	1	4,000 0 0	
	Stock in trade valued at	,,	17,000 0 0	
	Loose Plant, Tools and Fittings, valued at	,,	5,000 0 0	
	Book Debts, £40,390, subject to a deduction of 5 per cent.	,,	38,370 0 0	
			£64,370 0 0	
1894 Sept. 30	To Balance brought forward to be paid off by 7 equal annual instalments from 4 August 1894, and to carry interest at 5 per cent.	fo.	34,970 0 0	
1895 Aug. 4	To Income, 1 year's interest on £34,970 at 5 per cent., less I. T. £58 5s. 8d.	10		1,690 4 4
1896 Aug. 4	To Income—1 year's interest on £29,975 at 5 per cent., less I. T. £49 19s. 2d.	10		1,448 15 10
1897 Aug. 4	To Income—1 year's interest on £24,980 at 5 per cent., less I. T. £41 12s. 8d.	10		1,207 7 4
1898 Mar. 31	To Income—Proportion of 1 year's interest on £19,985, 239 days at 5 per cent., less I. T. £21 16s. 8d.	10		633 0 0
			£34,970 0 0	£4,979 7 6

52
Cr.

TRADE ACCOUNT) IN ACCOUNT WITH THE
ARTHUR BRADSHAW, ESQ.

		fo.	Principal			Income		
			£	s	d	£	s	d
1894								
Aug. 4	By Legacies—Part of Testator's Capital specifically bequeathed to you	9	10,000	0	0			
,,	By Legacies—Goodwill of trade valued for probate at 1 year's profits on the average of 3 preceding years, £4,000 specifically bequeathed to you	9	4,000	0	0			
Sept. 30	By Debts — Amount due from Testator discharged by you	8	15,400	0	0			
	By Balance carried forward to be paid off by 7 equal annual instalments from 4 August 1894, and to carry interest at 5 per cent.		34,970	0	0			
			£64,370	0	0			

NOTE.—Vouchers for the debts discharged, £15,400, were produced to the executor's accountants.

		fo.	£	s	d	£	s	d
1895								
Aug. 4	By Cash—One-seventh of £34,970	20	4,995	0	0			
,,	By Cash—1 year's interest ..	,,				1,690	4	4
1896								
Aug. 4	By Cash—One-seventh of £34,970	,,	4,995	0	0			
,,	By Cash—1 year's interest ..	,,				1,448	15	10
1897								
Aug. 4	By Cash—One-seventh of £34,970	,,	4,995	0	0			
,,	By Cash—1 year's interest ..	,,				1,207	7	4
1898								
Mar. 31	By Arthur James Bradshaw—Part of Share of Residue applied in satisfaction of the balance due upon this Account for Principal and Interest ..	62	19,985	0	0	633	0	0
			£34,970	0	0	£4,979	7	6

53
Dr.   ARTHUR JAMES BRADSHAW,

							fo.	£	s	d
1895										
Sept. 4	To Cash ..	..	..	..	..	..	20	498	15	7
1898										
Mar. 31	To Cash ..	..	..	..	..	..	,,	899	18	3
								£1,398	13	10

54
Dr.   EMILY BRADSHAW,

		fo.	£	s	d
1898					
Mar. 31	To Emily Bradshaw Maintenance Account— Transfer of amount allowed for maintenance	55	700	0	0
,,	To Emily Bradshaw Share of Residue and Legacy Account—Transfer of balance of Income to this day when she attained 21 years	63	698	13	9
			£1,398	13	9

55
Dr.   EMILY BRADSHAW (MAINTENANCE ACCOUNT) IN ACCOUNT WITH

		fo.	£	s	d
1895					
Aug. 4	To Cash—Per James Bradshaw, 1 year's maintenance	20	200	0	0
1898					
Feb. 4	To Cash—Per James Bradshaw, 2½ years' maintenance	,,	500	0	0
			£700	0	0

INCOME ACCOUNT.   *Cr.* [53]

1895		fo.	£	s	d
Aug. 4	By Income—One-half share of the balance of Income to date	10	498	15	7
1898					
Mar. 31	By Income—One-half of the balance of Income to date	10	899	18	3
			£1,398	13	10

INCOME ACCOUNT.   *Cr.* [54]

1895		fo.	£	s	d
Aug. 4	By Income— One-half of the balance of Income to date	10	498	15	6
1898					
Mar. 31	By Income — One-half of the balance of Income to date	10	899	18	3
			£1,398	13	9

THE ESTATE OF THE LATE ARTHUR BRADSHAW, ESQ.   *Cr.* [55]

1898		fo.	£	s	d
Mar. 31	By Emily Bradshaw Income Account— Transfer of amount allowed for maintenance	54	700	0	0
			£700	0	0

F

60
Dr. EMILY BRADSHAW (LEGACY ACCOUNT) IN ACCOUNT WITH

1898		fo.	£	s	d
Mar. 31	To Emily Bradshaw Share of Residue and Legacy Account—Transfer of Legacy and accumulations of income arising therefrom to this day when she attained 21 years of age	63	11,024	13	4
			£11,024	13	4

61
Dr. DUTY ON RESIDUE IN ACCOUNT WITH THE ESTATE

1895		fo.				£	s	d
Jan. 31	To Cash, viz.:—*For Arthur James Bradshaw*—							
	Duty on Goodwill of Testator's Trade ..		120	0	0			
	Half-share of Residue ..		907	10	0			
	For Emily Bradshaw—							
	Half-share of Residue ..		907	10	0	1,935	0	0
						£1,935	0	0

62
Dr. ARTHUR JAMES BRADSHAW

1898		fo.	£	s	d
Mar. 31	To Arthur James Bradshaw—Purchase of Trade Account, Transfer of Balance due upon that Account..	52	20,618	0	0
,,	To Duty on Residue—Transfer of one Half-share	61	907	10	0
,,	To Cash—Balance of Share of Residue ..	20	4,898	6	10
			£26,423	16	10

THE ESTATE OF THE LATE ARTHUR BRADSHAW, ESQ.   60
                                                            Cr.

1894		fo.	£	s	d
Aug. 4	By Legacies—Legacy in trust	9	10,000	0	0
1896					
Aug. 4	By Income—1 year's interest from 4th August, 1895, on £10,000 at 4 per cent., less I. T. £13 6s. 8d.	10	386	13	4
1898					
Mar. 31	By Income—Interest to date on £10,000 at 4 per cent., less I. T. £22	,,	638	0	0
			£11,024	13	4

OF THE LATE ARTHUR BRADSHAW, ESQ.   61
                                                            Cr.

1895		fo.	£	s	d
Jan. 31	By Cash—Per Arthur James Bradshaw— Duty on Goodwill	20	120	0	0
1898					
Mar. 31	By Arthur James Bradshaw— Transfer of Duty on Half-share of Residue..	62	907	10	0
,,	By Emily Bradshaw— Transfer of Duty on Half-share of Residue	63	907	10	0
			£1,935	0	0

SHARE OF RESIDUE.   62
                                                            Cr.

1898		fo.	£	s	d
Mar. 31	By Principal—One Half-share of Residue	1	26,423	16	10
			£26,423	16	10

F 2

63
Dr.   EMILY BRADSHAW,

1898		fo.	£	s	d
Mar. 31	To Duty on Residue—Transfer of Duty on Half-share of Residue	61	907	10	0
,,	To Testamentary Expenses — Settlement Estate Duty on Legacy of £10,000, and on £28,765, her one Half-share of the total Estate, less Legacies, as shown by the Executor's Affidavit for Inland Revenue	6	287	0	0
,,	To Balance carried forward, being Legacy of £10,000 and Income thereof, and Half-share of Residue, held in trust, to pay the income to her for life, and, after her death, for her children, if any, in equal shares, and failing issue to Arthur James Bradshaw		36,952	14	0
			£38,147	4	0

SHARE OF RESIDUE AND LEGACY. $\overset{63}{Cr.}$

1898		fo.	£	s	d
Mar. 31	By Principal—One Half-share of Residue	1	26,423	16	11
,,	By Emily Bradshaw — Legacy Account— Transfer of Legacy of £10,000 and Income thereof to this day, when she attained 21 years	60	11,024	13	4
,,	By Emily Bradshaw — Income Account— Transfer of Balance of her share of Income to this day, when she attained 21 years	54	698	13	9
			£38,147	4	0

1898	.	fo	£	s	d
Mar 31ᵐ	By Balance brought forward, being Legacy of £10,000 and Income thereof, and half-share of Residue, held in trust, to pay the income to her for life, and, after her death, for her children, if any, in equal shares, and failing issue to Arthur James Bradshaw . . .		£36,952	14	0

FORM No. 3.　INLAND REVENUE.　[FORM OF RESIDUARY ACCOUNT.]

☞ Here state the Name and Address of the person who forwards this Account.

JAMES & SON, Chartered Accountants,
59 Gresham Street, London, E.C.

All Personal Estate, and also, where mixed up with the Personal Estate, all Moneys arising from the sale, mortgage, or other disposition of all Real Estate directed by Will to be sold, &c., are to be accounted for upon this Form, for the purpose of having the Legacy Duty assessed pursuant to the Legacy Duty Act, 1796 (36 Geo. III. c. 52); the Legacy Duty Act, 1805 (45 Geo. III. c. 28); the Stamp Act, 1815 (55 Geo. III. c. 184), and the Finance Act, 1894 (57 & 58 Vict. c. 30), and the Succession Duty pursuant to the Customs and Inland Revenue Act, 1888 (51 & 52 Vict. c. 8).

Where the Personal Estate is not chargeable with Legacy Duty, the proceeds of sale of Real Estate directed to be sold should be accounted for upon the Form No. 8; as also where moneys arising from the sale of Real Estate do not form part of the General Estate but are separately given.

Where Temporary Estate Duty under the Customs and Inland Revenue Act, 1889 (52 & 53 Vict. c 7), s. 6, is payable on any property included in this account, a separate Statement of the value of such property on Form No. 13 should be delivered.

The account when filled up in duplicate should be presented personally, or by an agent, at the Legacy and Succession Duty Office, Somerset House, London, W.C., or it may be sent there through the Post from an address outside the Metropolitan Postal District.

☞ OBSERVE.—Money should not be remitted until the account has been delivered by the parties, and the amount payable and the mode of payment have been notified to them.

DIRECTIONS.

Executors and Administrators, before the Retainer of any part of the Property to their own use, are to deliver the particulars thereof, and pay the duty thereon within 14 days after, under the Penalty of treble the value of the Duty.

All Rents, Dividends, Interest, and Profits arising from the Personal Estate of the Deceased, or from the Real Estate directed by Will to be sold, &c., subsequently to the time of the death, and all accretions thereon down to the time of computing the Duty, must be considered as part of the Estate, and be accounted for accordingly.

REGISTER.　　No. 150 of the Year 1894.　　Folio 520.　　Affidavit.

An Account ‡ of the Personal Estate, and of Moneys arising out of the Real Estate of Arthur Bradshaw, late of the Atlas Works, Bermondsey, and of No. 1001 Hampstead Road, London, N., Mechanical Engineer who died on the fourth day of August One thousand eight hundred and ninety-four exhibited by *James Bradshaw and Charles Drury both of No. 100 Great George Street, Westminster, the Executors of the Deceased, (or) Trustees of the Real Estate directed by the Will to be sold, &c., acting under the Will of the Deceased, proved in the Principal Registry of the Probate Division of the High Court of Justice, on the fourteenth day of August 1894.

‡Please read the Instructions printed above.

*Here state the Name and Address of the Executor or Administrator

DESCRIPTION OF PROPERTY.	Date of Sale, if Sold.	No. 1. Money received and Property converted into Money.			No. 2. Value of Property not converted into Money.		
		£	s	d	£	s	d
Cash in the House		20	17	6			
Cash at the Bankers		1,080	12	0			
†Furniture, Plate, Linen, China, Books, Pictures					1,800	0	0
Wearing Apparel, Jewels, and Ornaments .... } Specifically bequeathed to Widow of Testator							
†Wine and other Liquors }							
†Horses and Carriages, Farming Stock, and Implements of Husbandry }	30th Sept. 1894	161	10	0			
†Stock in Trade					22,000	0	0
†Goodwill, &c., of Trade or Business					4,000	0	0
Life Assurance Policies					5,360	0	0
Rents due at the death of the deceased		193	6	8	43	1	6
Mortgages and Interest due at the Death		79	17	5	6,000	0	0
Bonds, Bills, Notes, and Interest due at the Death							
Book and other Debts		15,400	0	0	1,004	12	8
Canal Shares, viz.					22,970	0	0
Railway Shares, viz.:—£5,000 Consolidated Guaranteed 4 % Stock of the L. & N.W. Rly. Co., at £142 }							
Other Shares, viz.					7,100	0	0
The Stocks or other Securities of British Colonies, viz. }							
Ships, or Shares of Ships							
Carried forward		16,936	3	7	70,277	14	2

Money and Property converted into Money are to be inserted in Column No. 1, and the date when converted into Money is to be affixed.

† Property not converted into Money is to be valued at the time the Account is rendered, and its value so ascertained inserted in Column No. 2, and Inventories and proper Valuations must be produced

As to apportionment of Rents and other income see the Apportionment Act 1870 (33 & 34 Vict. c. 35).

The Shares not converted into Money are to be valued at the market price of the day on which the Account is dated. If there be Shares in many Companies it may be convenient to insert the total amount or value in this Account, and annex a Statement of the particular Shares.

Note.	DESCRIPTION OF PROPERTY.	Date of Sale, if Sold.	No. 1. Money received and Property converted into Money.	No. 2. Value of Property not converted into Money.
If there should not be room in this Form for the particulars of any description of Property, the total only of the amount or value of such Property is to be inserted here, and the particulars are to be stated on a separate paper. The Stocks unconverted are to be valued at the market price of the day on which the Account is dated.	Brought forward............		£ s d 16,936 3 7	£ s d 70,277 14 2
	Price of Stocks.			
	Exchequer Bills...........£			
	Bank Stock ....£			
	East India Stock ....£			
	East India Bonds.........£			
	3 per cent. Consols ......£			
	3 per cent. reduced ......£			
	New 3 per cents. ....£			
	2¾ per cent. Consols......£			
	2¾ per cent. reduced......£			
	2½ per cent. reduced......£			
	Dividends on the above Stocks Due at the Death............			
	The Stocks or Public Securities of Foreign States, viz.			
	Property which the Testator had power to appoint as he thought fit, viz.			
	Property not comprised within the above description, viz. ..			
	Real Estate and Leasehold Estates directed to be sold, as per statement of particulars annexed			
	Four Leasehold Houses in the New Road Willesden held for an unexpired term of 95 years from Ladyday 1894, at an annual ground rent of £40. This property is let upon annual tenancies at a gross rental of £400 per annum, and is valued by Messrs. Smith & Johnson at £6,500.			6,500 0 0
	Carried forward........			76,777 14 2

DESCRIPTION OF PROPERTY.	Date of Sale, if Sold.	No. 1. Money received and Property converted into Money.			No. 2. Value of Property not converted into Money.		
		£	s	d	£	s	d
Brought forward..........					76,777	14	2
„ OBSERVE. Was the deceased possessed for life or otherwise of any *Real or Leasehold* Estates, other than those brought into this Account? Reply, No. — Freehold House, No. 1001 Hampstead Road, occupied by Testator. The gross assessment is £230, and the property is valued at £4,443 15s. 0d.					4,443	15	0
(Insert the Total of Column No. 1 in Column No. 2)					16,936	3	7
Total of Property....£					98,157	12	9

PAYMENTS.

	£	s	d
*A Statement of these Deductions, signed by the Executor or Administrator, is to be annexed.			
Probate or Administration			
Funeral Expenses			
Expenses attending Executorship or Administration..........			
* Debts on Simple Contract, Rent and Taxes, Wages, &c., due at the Death of the Deceased, as per Statement annexed	5,300	0	0
	30	0	0
	775	0	0
† Here state the particulars of any other lawful payments and of the Funds or other securities purchased, and when. Debts on Mortgage, with Interest (if any) due at the Death	15,489	11	9
* Debts on Bonds and other Securities, with ditto..........	„	„	„
Pecuniary Legacies, as per Statement annexed Mary Bradshaw at	„	„	„
† The Legacies £10,000 each to Arthur James Bradshaw and Emily Bradshaw and of the goodwill of the business to Arthur James Bradshaw are treated as part of Residue. purchased on the of	500	0	0

(Deduct the Total of the Payments from the Total of the Property).....£ 22,094 11 9

Net Amount of Property carried forward.......... £ 76,063 1 0

To show BALANCE of CASH, if any.
Total of Column No. 1............£16,936 3 7
Total of Payments £22,094 11 9

Cash Account..£ „ „ „

No. 3.

INTEREST, DIVIDENDS, RENTS, &c., SINCE THE DEATH.

Note.— Upon reversions falling in, state the date of the death of the Tenant for life.

Separate Papers are to be annexed to the Account to show how these Totals are made up.

* If the Cash balance has borne interest, the actual amount earned should be brought in. If it has not, but could have done so, interest at 3 per cent. per annum should be brought in.

	£	s	d
Net amount of Property brought forward....	76,063	1	0
Rents of Real and Leasehold Estates directed to be Sold to the time of Sale, if Sold; if not, to the date of this Account	135	4	7
Dividend on the Stocks and Funds Sold to the time of Sale, and of those remaining Unsold, including the last Dividends			
Interest on Exchequer Bills Sold or Paid off to the time of Sale or Payment, and of those remaining Unsold, to the date of this Account	78	5	7
Interest on Bonds, Mortgages, and other Securities Paid off, to the Day of Payment, and of those outstanding, to the date of this Account			
* Interest on £ being the balance of Cash in Hand as ca...	55	13	3
Income of Canal, Railway, and other Shares, to the time of Sale, and of those remaining Unsold, and on other Property, yielding an Income not included in any of the above Items, to the date of this Account			
The value of the Benefit accruing to the Executor or other Person entitled to the Residue from the Interest of Money or Dividends of Stock retained to answer vested or contingent Legacies, payable at a future day without the Intermediate Interest or Dividends			
Total........	£76,332	4	5

PAYMENTS OUT OF INTEREST, &c.

	£	s	d
Interest on Mortgages, Bonds, and other Securities, due from the Estate			
Interest on Pecuniary Legacies			
Payments on account of Annuities, 5 months at £1,200 per annum	500	0	0
Other Payments, if any, viz.			
(Deduct the Total Amount of these Payments from the foregoing Total)........	500	0	0
Balance carried forward....	£75,832	4	5

	£	s	d
Brought forward....	75,832	4	5

DEDUCTIONS FROM RESIDUE.

	£	s	d
Debts still due from the Estate			
Retained to pay outstanding Legacies	750	0	0
Value of an annuity of £1,200, bequeathed to Testator's Widow, whose age on the 3rd December 1894 was 69 years	8,462	8	0
Value of the widow's life interest in Freehold House, Hampstead Road, being equal to an annuity of £230.	1,620	18	0
Value of widow's life interest in Household Furniture, valued at £1,800, equal at 4 per cent. to an annuity of £72	507	15	0
Total Deductions....	£11,341	1	0
Net Residue........	£64,491	3	5

Deduct any portion of the Residue not liable to Duty, or for which Duty is paid on separate Receipts, viz. ....

Residue on which Duty is chargeable	£64,491	3	5

DECLARATION.

No. 1.

For use in all cases except as in No. 2.

We do declare that the foregoing is a just and true Account, and I (or) We offer to pay the sum of £1,935 for the Legacy Duty, at the rate of 3 per cent. upon the sum of £64,491, being (1) *the whole of the* said Residue and Moneys to which

No. 2.

For use only where the Testator died after 30th June, 1888, and before 2nd August, 1894, and then only where the Residue comprises Real Estate directed to be sold as well as Personal Estate.

I (or) We do declare that the foregoing is a just and true Account, and I (or) We offer to pay the sum of £ , of which £   is the *Legacy* Duty at   per cent. on £   the proportion representing Personal Estate, and £   is the *Succession* Duty at   per cent. on £   the proportion representing Real Estate to which

We are entitled and which we intend to retain to our own use, and for the use of (2) *Arthur James Bradshaw and Emily Bradshaw, being* (3) *descendants of a brother of the Deceased.*
Dated this *5th* day of *January* 1895.

(Here sign the Account) James Bradshaw,
Charles Drury.

A Schedule of Particulars of these deductions to be annexed.

(1) State whether this Sum is the whole or what part of the Residue. (2) Insert the Christian and Surnames of the Residuary Legatees or next of kin, and (3) their Relationship or Consanguinity, in the words of the Act, as set forth on the other side.

This portion to be used with either form of declaration.

Rates of Legacy Duty payable on Legacies, Annuities, and Residues, by the Stamp Act, 1815 (55 Geo. III. c. 184), and the Customs and Inland Revenue Act, 1888 (51 & 52 Vict. c. 8).

NOTE.—If the Deceased died on or after the 1st June 1881, every Pecuniary Legacy or Residue or Share of Residue, although not of the amount or value of £20, is chargeable with Duty; Customs and Inland Revenue Act, 1881 (44 & 45 Vict. c. 12), s. 42.

The Description of the Residuary Legatee, or next of Kin, is to be in the following words of the Act.

	On Real Estate, if the Deceased died *before* 1st July, 1888, or if Estate Duty under the Finance Act, 1894 has been paid upon the property, and on Personal Estate.	On Apportioned Value of Real Estate where Deceased died *on or after* 1st July, 1888, and Estate Duty under the Finance Act, 1894, has not been paid upon the property.
* Children of the Deceased, and their Descendants, or the Father or Mother, or any Lineal Ancestor of the Deceased, or the Husbands or Wives of any such Persons	1 per Cent	1½ per Cent.
Brothers and Sisters of the Deceased and their Descendants, or the Husbands or Wives of any such Persons	3 do.	4½ do.
Brothers and Sisters of the Father or Mother of the Deceased, and their Descendants, or the Husbands or Wives of any such Persons	5 do.	6½ do.
Brothers and Sisters of a Grandfather or Grandmother of the Deceased, and their Descendants, or the Husbands or Wives of any such Persons	6 do.	7½ do.
Any Person in any other Degree of Collateral Consanguinity, or strangers in Blood to the Deceased	10 do.	11½ do.

* Persons otherwise chargeable with Legacy Duty at the rate of 1 per cent. are exempt in respect of any Legacy, Residuo, or Share of Residue payable out of, or consisting of any Estate or Effects according to the value whereof duty shall have been paid on the Affidavit or Inventory, in conformity with the Customs and Inland Revenue Act, 1881, or where Estate Duty under the Finance Act, 1894 has been paid upon the value of the Property, and the same passes under the Deceased's Will or Intestacy.

The Husband or Wife of the Deceased is not subject to Legacy Duty.

Relations of the Husband or Wife of the Deceased are chargeable with Legacy Duty at the rate of 10 per cent. or 11½ per cent., as the case may be, unless themselves related in blood to the Deceased.

OBSERVE.—Interest at the rate of 3 per cent. per annum is chargeable upon Legacy and Succession Duty in arrear, under the provisions of the Finance Act, 1896 (59 & 60 Vict. c. 28), s. 18 (2).

Postage
Free

On Her Majesty's Service.

The Controller of Legacy and Succession Duties,

Somerset House,

London,

W C.

Total Duty.

For Official use only.]

ASSESSMENT.

The *Legacy Duty* on the } said Sum of........   £   ,,   at   Per cent. is £   ,,   ,,

Interest thereon   ..   ..   ..   ,,   ,,   ,,

     Total Legacy Duty £   ,,   ,,

The *Succession Duty* on } the said Sum of .....   £   ,,   at   per cent. is £   ,,   ,,

Interest thereon   ..   ..   ..   ,,   ,,   ,,

     Total Succession Duty £   ,,   ,,

£   ,,   ,,

SOMERSET HOUSE,
LONDON, W.C.,

   day of _____ 189

By the Commissioners,

Registrar.

RECEIPT FOR DUTY.

Received the   day of   189   , the Sum of

being the Amount mentioned in the above Assessment.

Registered,

£   ,,   ,,

pro Accountant.   pro. Cashier.

For Acct. and Compt.-Genl.
of Inland Revenue.

Accountancy and

Law Publications.

GEE & CO., PUBLISHERS,

34 MOORGATE ST., LONDON, E.C

The Accountant.

The Recognised Weekly Organ of Chartered Accountants

AND

Accountancy throughout the World.

Volumes Commence in January and July.

THE ACCOUNTANT is published weekly, in time for Friday evening's mail, and is the medium of communication between the members of the Institute of Chartered Accountants in England and Wales and Accountants generally throughout the World.

Contents :

LEADING ARTICLES.	LECTURES AND DEBATES ON
WEEKLY NOTES.	BOOKKEEPING, WITH
CORRESPONDENCE.	SPECIMENS OF ACCOUNTS.
CURRENT LAW.	AUDITING, LIQUIDATIONS, ETC.

AND

A "LAW REPORTS" SUPPLEMENT

which contains reports of all decisions of importance as to Administrations; Company Winding-up; Bankruptcies; Mercantile Law; and Partnerships.

Subscriptions :

Yearly .. 24/-	Half-Yearly .. 13/-	Post free, United Kingdom
,, .. 26/-	,, .. 14/	,, Abroad.

Payable in Advance

The Accountants' Journal.

(With which is Incorporated the Accountants Students' Journal.)

Annual Subscription 7/6 per annum post free.

ALTERATIONS AND IMPROVEMENTS. Many important Alterations and Improvements were introduced in Volume XXII., which commenced in May 1904.

CONTENTS. The general Contents of the paper are designed more especially to meet the requirements of **Accountant Students,** and especially Examination Candidates. A Concise Summary of the effect of **all important legal decisions** appears in each number. At least one original Article appears in each issue dealing with some matter of interest to Accountant Students.

PRIZE COMPETITION. Arrangements have been made for a **Serial Competition,** that is, one extending through several numbers, and a Prize awarded to the best Answers given on Questions of general interest.

STUDENTS' SOCIETIES. Each Students' Society has been invited to nominate a contributor to send monthly a short account of what is being done by his Society; and it is intended to give as much freedom as possible to the matters that may be discussed thereunder, so that within reasonable limits each Society may consider that it has a portion of the *Journal* at its own disposal to discuss such matters as it may consider of importance.

CONTRIBUTIONS. All readers are invited to make use of the Correspondence column; and careful consideration will be given to all original Articles forwarded for insertion, which, if approved, will be paid for at the usual rates, unless the author wishes them to appear under his name, in which case no payment can be made.

VOLUMES. Back numbers of the Journal (bound, half-calf, gold lettered) can be obtained, Vols. I.-XII. price **7/6** each or **72/-** for the set of 12; and Vols. XIII. to XXI. price **8/6** each.

SUBSCRIPTION ORDER FORM.

Date...............................

To Messrs. Gee & Co.,
    34 Moorgate St., London, E.C.

    Please supply "The Accountants' Journal," monthly, until further notice. Enclosed is remittance for..................................being the amount of..................year's Subscription in advance.

    Name...

    Address..

    ....

The Accountants' Library.

This important Series of Handbooks, which is being issued monthly, deals with Systems of Bookkeeping suitable for all classes of undertakings.

The following Volumes (which complete the first series) have already been issued.

	NET PRICE s d		NET PRICE s d
I.—Bank Bookkeeping and Accounts (MEELBOOM)	5 0	XI.—Polytechnic Accounts (MARSHALL)	3 6
II.—Auctioneers' Accounts (DICKSEE)	3 6	XII.—Solicitors' Accounts (DICKSEE)	3 6
III.—Builders' Accounts (WALBANK)	3 6	XIII.—Pawnbrokers' Accounts (THORNTON & MAY)	3 6
IV.—Agricultural Accounts and Income Tax (MEATS)	5 0	XIV.—Engineers' and Ship-builders' Accounts (BURTON) ..	3 6
V.—Theatre Accounts (CHANTREY)	3 6	XV.—Tramway Accounts (McCOLL) Triple Number ..	10 6
VI.—Co-operative Societies' Accounts (SUGDEN)	5 0	XVI.—Australian Mining Companies' Accounts (GODDEN & ROBERTSON)	3 6
VII.—Gas Accounts (THE EDITOR)	5 0	XVII.—Printers' Accounts (LAKIN-SMITH)	3 6
VIII.—Mineral Water Manufacturers' Accounts (LUND & RICHARDSON)	6	XVIII.—Medical Practitioners' Accounts (MAY)	3 6
IX.—Stockbrokers' Accounts (CALLAWAY)	6	XIX.—Water Companies' Accounts (KEY)	3 6
X.—Grain, Flour, Hay, and Seed Merchants' Accounts (JOHNSON)	3 6	XX.—Fishing Industry Accounts (WILLIAMSON)	3 6

To Subscribers these are published at the special rate of 2s. 6d. per volume (3s. 9d. per "Double" volume). Subscriptions can still be received at this reduced rate by those desirous of obtaining the whole Series, but the back volumes must be paid for *en bloc*. (£2 17s. 6d. for the first series; £2 10s. 0d. for the first 16 volumes of the second series.)

Subscribers who may not wish to acquire the whole of the back volumes may, however, commence their Subscription with Vol. XXI.

Single copies of any volume may be obtained at the ordinary rates as detailed above.

For Subscription Order Form see next page.

The Accountants' Library.

(SECOND SERIES)

SUBSCRIPTIONS are now invited for a Second Series of volumes which are being issued monthly in connection with this publication. The first sixteen issues (Vols. XXI. to XXXVI. of the whole Series) have now been published as follows :—

XXI.—MUNICIPAL ACCOUNTS. (ALLCOCK) Triple Number, 10/6

XXII.—UNDERWRITERS' ACCOUNTS. (SPICER & PEGLER) 3/6

XXIII.—JEWELLERS' ACCOUNTS. (ALLEN EDWARDS) Double Number, 5/-

XXIV.—MULTIPLE - SHOP ACCOUNTS. (HAZELIP) 3/6

XXV.—BUILDING SOCIETIES' ACCOUNTS. (GRANT-SMITH) 3/6

XXVI.—DEPRECIATION, RESERVES, AND RESERVE FUNDS. (DICKSEE) 3/6

XXVII.—QUARRY ACCOUNTS. (IBOTSON) 3/6

XXVIII.—FRIENDLY SOCIETIES' ACCOUNTS. (FURNIVAL JONES) 5/-

XXIX.—ELECTRIC LIGHTING ACCOUNTS. (JOHNSON) 5/-

XXX.—FRAUD IN ACCOUNTS. (EDITOR) 3/6

XXXI.—DRAPERS' ACCOUNTS. (RICHARDSON) 3/6

XXXII.—WINE MERCHANTS' ACCOUNTS. (SABIN) Double Number, 5/-

XXXIII.—DAIRY ACCOUNTS. (ROWLAND) 3/6

XXXIV.—BRICKMAKERS' ACCOUNTS. (FOX) 3/6

XXXV.—TIMBER MERCHANTS' ACCOUNTS. (SMITH) 3/6

XXXVI.—INSURANCE COMPANIES' ACCOUNTS. (TYLER) Triple Number, 10/6

It is expected that the two Series will comprise about 50 volumes in all.

THE NEXT VOLUMES OF THE SERIES WILL BE :—

XXXVII.—HOTEL ACCOUNTS, by LAWRENCE R. DICKSEE, M.Com., F.C.A. (Ready Feb. 1905.)

XXXVIII.—COTTON SPINNERS' ACCOUNTS. By WILLIAM MOSS, F.C.A.

Arrangements have already been made for the following subjects to be dealt with (but not necessarily in the order stated). Applications are, however, invited from competent authors desirous of undertaking further suitable subjects :—

Domestic Tradesmen's Accounts.

Laundry Accounts.

Publishers' Accounts.

School Accounts.

Shipping Accounts

Tailors' Accounts.

Trustees', Liquidators', and Receivers' Accounts.

SUBSCRIPTION ORDER FORM.

To Messrs. GEE & CO.

Dear Sirs,—I request you to forward to me <u>* Vols. I. to XX.</u> *of* <u>Vols. XXI. to end</u> <u>whole of the Volumes</u> *"* THE ACCOUNTANTS' LIBRARY *" as published, and I hereby agree to pay for the same at the special subscription rate of 2s. 6d. net for each single Volume, and 3s. 9d. net for each Volume issued as a "Double Number."*

Name ....

Date.................... *Address* ....

* Strike out two lines, in accordance with your requirements.

Vols. I., II., III., IV., V., VI., VII., VIII., and IX.   *Price 12/6 net*
each, except Vol. III., price 10/6 net, or 90/- the set.

Bound in Cloth, and Gold Lettered.

Terms of Subscription, 3/6 per annum, Including Index Biennially.

The Accountants' Manual

A most valuable fund of information concerning various points of Practice
and Law Relating to the Profession is that contained in the Questions and Answers
of the Institute Examinations.

The above Volumes comprise the back numbers of the Questions and Answers with
copious and carefully-prepared Indices.   By this means an extremely valuable mass of
information, which for some time had only been available to the Student for Examination
purposes, is thrown open to practitioners; and the series— comprising a **complete
professional code** that will be in daily request—should find a place on the shelf of
every member of the Profession.

Throughout the Series, the Answers have been written with the utmost care, and
the views of specialists have been obtained in all cases where there has been the
slightest doubt as to the correct practice. In the preparation of the Indices, the greatest
pains have been taken to frame them in accordance with the **requirements of
Chartered Accountants**, and all points of law that have been rendered obsolete by
recent legislation have not been indexed.

The Series forms one of the most valuable Contributions to the
literature of the Profession.

The first Volume comprises the Examination Questions and Answers from
December 1884 to June 1887 (both inclusive); the second Volume includes those
from December 1887 to June 1890; the third Volume comprises the Questions and
Answers from December 1890 to June 1892; the fourth Volume, the Questions and
Answers from December 1892 to June 1894; the fifth Volume, the Questions and
Answers from December 1894 to June 1896; the sixth Volume, the Questions and
Answers from December 1896 to June 1898; the seventh Volume, the Questions
and Answers from December 1898 to June 1900; the eighth Volume, the Questions
and Answers from December 1900 to June 1902; and the ninth Volume, the Questions
and Answers from December 1902 to June 1904 (both inclusive). The Questions
and Answers published after that date will form the succeeding Volumes, which
it is proposed to issue every other year.

To those who have subscribed for these Questions and Answers as and when
issued, the Indices will be supplied separately, price 2/6 each, and will thus be
obtainable for binding up with Subscribers' own sets. To Annual Subscribers, however, the Index is supplied free of further charge.

Recommended in the Official Syllabus for the C.P.A. Examinations (New York).

GEE & CO., Publishers, 34 Moorgate Street, London, E.C.

1905.

Accountancy and Law Publications.

						Pub. Price NET
Accountant, The.	Weekly	...	...	...	...	-/6
,,	,,	per annum, post free (U.K.)		...		24/-
,,	,,	do.	do.	Foreign	...	26/-
,,	,,	Binding Cases	...	...	...	2/6
,,	,,	File Cases	...	.	...	3/6
Accountants' Journal.	Monthly	...	...		...	-/9
,,	,,	Per annum (U.K.)		...		7/6
,,	,,	do.	Foreign		...	8/6
,,	,,	Binding Cases	...		...	2/6
,,	**and Bookkeeper's Vade-Mecum.**					
	(Whatley)	...	...	...	...	7/6
,,	**Assistant.** (Beckett)	...	...	...		6/-
,,	**Code**	...	...	...	doz.	5/-
,,	**Compendium.** (Dawson) (2nd Edition)					21/-
,,	**Diary.** I.	(Foolscap 1 day to page)			...	8/-
,,	,, II.	(,, 2 ,,)			...	3/6
,,	,, III.	(,, 3 ,,)			...	1/6
,,	,, III.A	(,, 3 ,,)			...	2/-
,,	,, IV.&IV.F.(8vo.	1 ,,)			..	5/-
,,	,, V.	(,, 2 ,,)			...	2/6
,,	**Manual.** Vols. I. to IX.,		...	each		12/6
,,	,, except Vol. III.		...		...	10/6
,,	,, The set of 9 Vols.		...		...	90/-
Advanced Accounting.	(Dicksee)	...	...		...	21/-
Agricultural Accounts.	(Meats)	...	...		...	5/-
Ante-Audit.	...	...	...	...	... each	1/-
,,	...	...	...	...	... ½-doz.	5/6
,,	...	...	...	...	... doz.	10/-
Auctioneers' Accounts.	(Dicksee)	...		...	...	3/6
Audit Note Books I. & II.,	each -/6; doz. **5/-**; 100					40/-
,, ,, **III.**	...	...	each **2/-**; doz.			20/-
				50 **70/-**; 100		110/-
Auditing.	(Dicksee) (6th Edition)	...	...		...	21/-
Australian Mining Companies' Accounts.						
(Godden & Robertson)		...	...	...	...	3/6

GEE & CO., 34 MOORGATE ST., LONDON, E.C.

	Pub. Price NET
Bank Bookkeeping and Accounts. (Meelboom) (2nd Edition)	5/-
Bankruptcy. (Stevens) (2nd Edition)	7/6
,, **Time Table.**	-/6
,, **Trustee's Estate Book.** (Dicksee) ... each 4/-, doz.	40/-
,, **Trustees, Liquidators, and Receivers, Law of.** (Willson)	5/-
Bookkeeping, Antiquity of. (Heaps)	1/-
,, **Elementary.** (Day)	1/-
,, **Elements of.** (Streeter)	1/6
,, **Exercises.** (Dicksee)	3/6
,, **for Accountant Students.** (Dicksee)	10/6
,, ,, **Company Secretaries.** (Dicksee)	3/6
,, ,, **Publishers.** (Allen)	2/6
,, ,, **Retail Traders.** (Findlay) ...	3/-
,, ,, ,, **Record Book.** (Findlay)	4/-
,, ,, **Solicitors.** (Hodsoll)	3/6
,, ,, **Technical Classes and Schools.** (Clarke)	2/6
,, ,, **Principles of.** (Carlill)	3/6
Brickmakers' Accounts. (Fox)	3/6
Builders' Accounts. (Walbank) (2nd Edition) ...	3/6
Building Societies' Accounts. (Grant-Smith) ...	3/6
,, **Society Table and Loan Calculations.** (Johnson.)	1/-
Chartered Accountants' Charges. (Pixley) (3rd Edition)	10/6
Companies Act, 1900. (Reid)	1/-
,, ,, ,, **Duties of Auditors under**	1/-
Company Secretary. (Fox) (4th Edition) ...	25/-
,, **Winding-up Time Table**	-/6
Compendium, Accountants'. (Dawson) (2nd Edition)	21/-
Co-operative Societies' Accounts. (Sugden) ...	5/-
Cost Accounts of an Engineer and Iron-founder. (Best)	2/6

	Pub. Price NET
Dairy Accounts. (Rowland)	3/6
Depreciation, Reserves, and Reserve Funds. (Dicksee)	3/6
,, **Tables.** (Dicksee)	1/-
Drapers' Accounts. (Richardson)	3/6
Electric Lighting Accounts. (Johnson)	5/-
Engineers' and Shipbuilders' Accounts. (Burton)	3/6
Errors in Balancing. (2nd Edition)	1/-
Examination Guide, Intermediate. (Nixon) ...	3/6
,, ,, **Final.** (Nixon)	5/-
,, **Papers (Questions & Answers)** June and December in each year, each ...	2/6
Examinations, Chartered Accountants', How to Prepare for. (Carlill)	1/6
Executorship Accounts. (Whinney) (2nd Edition)	7/6
,, ,, (Caldicott) (3rd Edition)	3/6
,, ,, **Student's Guide to.** (Carter)	3/6
Factory Accounts. (Garcke & Fells) (5th Edition)	7/6
Farm Accounts. (Woodman)	1/-
Fishing Industry Accounts. (Williamson) ...	3/6
Forms of Accounts. (Johnston)	2/6
Fraud in Accounts	3/6
Friendly Societies' Accounts. (Furnival Jones) ...	5/-
Gas Accounts	5/-
Goodwill. (Dicksee) (2nd Edition)	3/6
Grain, Hay, &c., Accounts. (Johnson)	3/6
Hire-Purchase Wagon Trade, &c., Bookkeeping and Accounts for. (Johnson)	1/6
Income Tax Practice, Guide to. (Murray & Carter) (3rd Edition)	10/-
Insurance Companies' Accounts. (Tyler)	10/6
Inwood's Tables	8/-
Jewellers' Accounts. (Allen Edwards)	5/-
Lexicon for Trustees in Bankruptcy, &c. Bound Boards. (Dawson)	3/6
List of Members. (Institute of Chartered Accountants)	2/-

	Pub. Price NET
Medical Practitioners' Accounts. (May)	3/6
Metric System. (Streeter)	1/-
Mineral Water Manufacturers' Accounts. (Lund & Richardson)	3/6
Multiple-Shop Accounts. (Hazelip)	3/6
Municipal Accounts. (Allcock)	10/6
,, Finance for Students	2/6
,, Internal Audit. (Collins)	3/6
Newspaper Accounts. (Norton & Feasey) ...	10/-
Office Rules and Regulations ... ... doz.	10/6
Partnership Accounts. (Child)	2/6
Pawnbrokers' Accounts. (Thornton & May) ...	3/6
Polytechnic Accounts. (Calder Marshall) ...	3/6
Printers' Accounts. (Lakin-Smith)	3/6
Professional Accountants. (Worthington) ...	2/6
Publishers' Accounts. (Allen)	2/6
Quarry Accounts. (Ibotson)	3/6
Retail Traders, Account Book for. (Day) ...	5/-
Shopkeepers' Accounts. (Quin) (2nd Edition) ...	2/6
Solicitors' Accounts. (Dicksee)	3/6
Stamp Duties and Receipts, Handbook to. (Lakin-Smith)	2/6
Stockbrokers' Accounts. (Callaway)	3/6
Student's Guide to Accountancy	2/6
Theatre Accounts. (Chantrey)	3/6
Timber Merchants' Accounts. (Smith)	3/6
Tramway Accounts. (McColl)	10/6
Trial Balance Book, "Handy" each -/6; doz.	5/-
Trustees, Liquidators, and Receivers, Law of. (Willson)	5/-
Underwriters' Accounts. (Spicer & Pegler) ...	3/6
Vade-Mecum, Accountant's and Bookkeeper's. (Whatley)	7/6
Van de Linde's Bookkeeping. (2nd Edition) ...	7/6
Water Companies' Accounts. (Key)	3/6
Wine and Spirit Merchants' Accounts. (Sabin) ...	5/-

COST ACCOUNTS OF AN ENGINEER AND IRON-FOUNDER, THE. Price 2s. 6d. net. By J. W. BEST,

F.C.A. The first portion deals with the Engineering and the second with the Foundry Department, and numerous forms of books and accounts are given and explained.

COMPARATIVE DEPRECIATION TABLES. Price

1s. net. By LAWRENCE R. DICKSEE, M.Com., F.C.A.

Containing a full set of Tables, showing the practical effect of providing for depreciation on the Fixed Instalment and the Fixed Percentage methods, and discussing their respective advantages.

DEPRECIATION, RESERVES, AND RESERVE FUNDS. Price 3s. 6d. net. 80 pages. By LAWRENCE R.

DICKSEE, M.Com., F.C.A.

This Work—which is Vol. XXVI. of "THE ACCOUNTANTS' LIBRARY" series—deals fully and impartially with the most Debatable and Important Subjects in connection with Accounts.

It is divided into Twelve Chapters, with a Complete Index, and is the most Exhaustive Work upon the subject that has yet been issued.

ELECTRIC LIGHTING ACCOUNTS. Price 5s. net.

Over 140 pages. By GEORGE JOHNSON, F.S.S., F.C.I.S.

This Work—which forms Vol. XXIX. of "THE ACCOUNTANTS' LIBRARY"—deals very fully with the Accounts of Electric Lighting Companies. It is divided into 18 Chapters, and contains a set of *pro formá* transactions. With a complete index.

EXAMINATION GUIDES.—INTERMEDIATE AND FINAL. Price 3s. 6d. and 5s. net respectively. By JOHN

G. NIXON, Junr., A.C.A.

These Books have been compiled in order to provide Accountant Students with a series of the Questions actually set at the Examinations of the Institute.

The Questions and Exercises include practically all those set from December 1893 to June 1903, and have been divided into sections. They have been arranged, according to subject, in alphabetical order; the dates when they were set being also given.

EXECUTORSHIP LAW AND ACCOUNTS. Second

Edition. Price 7s. 6d. Revised and brought up to date by FREDERICK WHINNEY, Junr., B.A., Barrister-at-Law, assisted by ARTHUR P. VAN NECK, M.A., Barrister-at-Law.

Containing an Epitome of a Will and a Set of Executorship Accounts. By ARTHUR F. WHINNEY, F.C.A.

EXECUTORSHIP ACCOUNTS. Third Edition. Price

3s. 6d. net. Revised under the FINANCE ACT and brought up to date. By O. H. CALDICOTT, F.C.A. Containing a COMPLETE SET of TRUST ACCOUNTS with explanatory text.

EXECUTORSHIP ACCOUNTS, STUDENT'S GUIDE TO. About

124 pages. Price 3s. 6d. net. By ROGER N. CARTER, F.C.A. (Senior Honours Institute Examination, June 1893), Joint Author with Mr. Adam Murray, F.C.A., of "A Guide to Income-Tax Practice."

FRAUD IN ACCOUNTS. Price 3s. 6d. This Work deals

with the methods of circumventing Frauds on the part of both Employees and Directors, and shows how they may be detected at an early date.

GAS ACCOUNTS (Vol. VII. of "THE ACCOUNTANTS

LIBRARY.") By the EDITOR. Price 5s. net.

This Work—which comprises 128 pages—deals fully with the Accounts of all classes of Gas undertakings. It contains an Introduction and Seven Chapters, and a Full Index is appended.

Lightning Source UK Ltd.
Milton Keynes UK
07 December 2010

164024UK00006B/26/P

Bond
No.1 for exam success

CU00690448

Verbal Reasoning

Assessment Papers

9–10 years

Book 2

OXFORD
UNIVERSITY PRESS

Great Clarendon Street, Oxford, OX2 6DP, United Kingdom

Oxford University Press is a department of the University of Oxford.
It furthers the University's objective of excellence in research,
scholarship, and education by publishing worldwide. Oxford is
a registered trade mark of Oxford University Press in the UK and in
certain other countries

British Library Cataloguing in Publication Data
Data available

978-0-19-274034-2

10 9 8 7 6 5 4 3

Paper used in the production of this book is a natural, recyclable
product made from wood grown in sustainable forests.
The manufacturing process conforms to the environmental
regulations of the country of origin.

Printed in China

Acknowledgements

The publishers would like to thank the following for permissions to
use copyright material:

Page make-up: OKS Prepress, India
Cover illustrations: Lo Cole

Although we have made every effort to trace and contact all
copyright holders before publication this has not been possible in all
cases. If notified, the publisher will rectify any errors or omissions at
the earliest opportunity.

Links to third party websites are provided by Oxford in good faith
and for information only. Oxford disclaims any responsibility for
the materials contained in any third party website referenced in
this work.

Before you get started

What is Bond?

This book is part of the Bond Assessment Papers series for verbal reasoning, which provides a **thorough and progressive course in verbal reasoning** from ages six to twelve. It builds up reasoning skills from book to book over the course of the series.

What does this book cover and how can it be used to prepare for exams?

Verbal reasoning questions can be grouped into four distinct groups: sorting words, selecting words, anagrams, coded sequences and logic. *Verbal Reasoning 9–10 Book 1 and Book 2* practise a wide range of questions appropriate to the age group drawn from all these categories. The papers can be used both for general practice and as part of the run up to 11+ and other selective exams. One of the key features of Bond Assessment Papers is that each one practises **a very wide variety of skills and question types** so that children are always challenged to think – and don't get bored repeating the same question type again and again. We believe that variety is the key to effective learning. It helps children 'think on their feet' and cope with the unexpected: it is surprising how often children come out of verbal reasoning exams having met question types they have not seen before.

What does the book contain?

- **15 papers** – each one contains 65 questions.
- **Tutorial links throughout -** 📖 – this icon appears in the margin next to the questions. It indicates links to the relevant section in *How to do 11+ Verbal Reasoning*, our invaluable subject guide that offers explanations and practice for all core question types.
- **Scoring devices** – there are score boxes in the margins and a Progress Chart on page 60. The chart is a visual and motivating way for children to see how they are doing. It also turns the score into a percentage that can help decide what to do next.
- **Next Steps Planner** – advice on what to do after finishing the papers can be found on the inside back cover.
- **Answers** – located in an easily removed central pull-out section.

How can you use this book?

One of the great strengths of Bond Assessment Papers is their flexibility. They can be used at home, in school and by tutors to:
- set **timed formal practice** tests – allow about 40 minutes per paper. Reduce the suggested time limit by five minutes to practise working at speed.
- provide **bite-sized chunks** for regular practice
- **highlight strengths and weaknesses** in the core skills
- identify **individual needs**
- set **homework**
- follow a complete 11+ preparation strategy alongside *The Parents' Guide to the 11+* (see overleaf).

It is best to start at the beginning and work though the papers in order. If you are using the book as part of a careful run-in to the 11+, we suggest that you also have two other essential Bond resources close at hand:

How to do 11+ Verbal Reasoning: the subject guide that explains all the question types practised in this book. Use the cross-reference icons to find the relevant sections.

The Parents' Guide to the 11+: the step-by-step guide to the whole 11+ experience. It clearly explains the 11+ process, provides guidance on how to assess children, helps you to set complete action plans for practice and explains how you can use the *Verbal Reasoning 9–10 Book 1* and *Book 2* as part of a strategic run-in to the exam.

See the inside front cover for more details of these books.

What does a score mean and how can it be improved?

It is unfortunately impossible to predict how a child will perform when it comes to the 11+ (or similar) exam if they achieve a certain score on any practice book or paper. Success on the day depends on a host of factors, including the scores of the other children sitting the test. However, we can give some guidance on what a score indicates and how to improve it.

If children colour in the Progress Chart on page 60, this will give an idea of present performance in percentage terms. The Next Steps Planner inside the back cover will help you to decide what to do next to help a child progress. It is always valuable to go over wrong answers with children. If they are having trouble with any particular question type, follow the tutorial links to *How to do 11+ Verbal Reasoning* for step-by-step explanations and further practice.

Don't forget the website…!

Visit www.bond11plus.co.uk for lots of advice, information and suggestions on everything to do with Bond, the 11+ and helping children to do their best.

Paper 1

Underline the pair of words most similar in meaning.

Example   come, go   <u>roam, wander</u>   fear, fare

1 test, exam   learn, read   science, mathematics

2 melt, fade   dirty, clean   rot, decay

3 drink, water   eat, consume   join, attract

4 hard, rough   black, red   light, pale

5 extend, enlarge   side, back   easy, late

Underline the two words, one from each group, which are the most opposite in meaning.

Example   (dawn, <u>early</u>, wake)   (<u>late</u>, stop, sunrise)

6 (once, then, here)   (never, open, now)

7 (large, hairy, wild)   (tiny, untidy, cold)

8 (stretch, easy, loose)   (pull, tight, take)

9 (awake, dark, hollow)   (solid, open, confused)

10 (second, minute, first)   (hour, third, final)

Complete the following sentences by selecting the most sensible word from each group of words given in the brackets. Underline the words selected.

Example   The (<u>children</u>, books, foxes) carried the (houses, <u>books</u>, steps) home from the (greengrocer, <u>library</u>, factory).

11 The (farmer, teacher, shopkeeper) asked the (men, sheep, children) to eat their (shoes, lunches, flowers) sensibly.

12 Don't (try, remember, forget) (swimming, jumping, running) in such a strong (puddle, tide, night).

13 Why are those (boats, trees, cows) standing (huddled, wide, near) together in the (shop, ground, field)?

14 The (team, colour, home) scored a (peach, ball, goal) to win the (last, match, run).

15 James (rubbed, used, whisked) the (jumper, dessert, pencil) with a (hose, pound, fork).

Underline the two words which are made from the same letters.

Example TAP PET <u>TEA</u> POT <u>EAT</u>

16 SHADES   SHADOW   SHIELD   DASHES   SHINES

17 STARS   TEARS   STATE   TEASE   RATES

18 PEARS   STEER   SPEAR   PLEAT   TREAT

19 SHOVE   FLASH   FLESH   SHAVE   SHELF

20 LATER   STEEL   TRAIL   STEAL   LEAST

Find the four-letter word hidden at the end of one word and the beginning of the next word. The order of the letters may not be changed.

Example The children had bats and balls.   <u>sand</u>

21 He decided to have breakfast early that morning.   _____

22 The garage mechanic repaired her new car promptly.   _____

23 'Don't I get a hello any more?' asked Mum.   _____

24 He put a larger dynamo onto the old bicycle.   _____

25 This was a radical move for Professor Shirka.   _____

Find the letter which will end the first word and start the second word.

Example peac (<u>h</u>) ome

26 mal (__) scape

27 hos (__) eat

28 see (__) ade

29 tea (__) ota

30 soa (__) ure

Find and underline the two words which need to change places for each sentence to make sense.

Example She went to <u>letter</u> the <u>write</u>.

31 The motor lake roared across the calm boat.

32 You thought that she couldn't hear I.

33 The mechanic was repaired by the car.

34 Where is you think she do going?

35 The caged sea roared like a angry lion.

2

Fill in the missing letters. The alphabet has been written out to help you.

A B C D E F G H I J K L M N O P Q R S T U V W X Y Z

Example AB is to CD as PQ is to <u>RS</u>.

36 JK is to LM as RS is to _____.

37 GE is to DB as AY is to _____.

38 EF is to HI as KL is to _____.

39 T5 is to V7 as X9 is to _____.

40 XX is to YA as BB is to _____.

B 23

5

Which one letter can be added to the front of all of these words to make new words?

Example <u>c</u>are <u>c</u>at <u>c</u>rate <u>c</u>all

41 ___old ___read ___ait ___rand

42 ___and ___old ___oup ___hare

43 ___otion ___ay ___ould ___ore

44 ___our ___outh ___oung ___ell

45 ___live ___bate ___bout ___mend

B 12

5

Fill in the crosswords so that all the given words are included. You have been given one letter as a clue in each crossword.

B 19

46
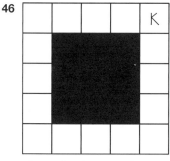
tiles, shark, start, knees

47
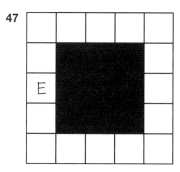
tries, fresh, front, heads

48
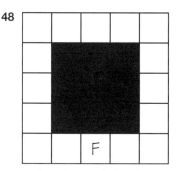
tufts, elves, aloft, above

49
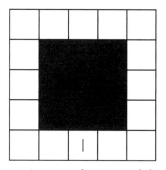
empty, round, rupee, daisy

50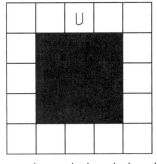

grand, gruel, dough, laugh

5

If the code for TRAVEL is $ * : £ − &, what are the codes for the following words?

B 24

51 REAL _____

52 TEAR _____

53 LEAVE _____

If the code for TRAIN is @ < ? > !, what do these codes stand for?

54 @ ? < _____

55 @ ? > ! @ _____

5

Underline the one word which **cannot be made** from the letters of the word in capital letters.

B 7

	Example	STATIONERY	stone	tyres	ration	<u>nation</u>	noisy
56	DETAILED		late	dated	laid	leaded	tamed
57	SUPERVISE		revise	revue	vipers	every	serve
58	COMPLICATED		laced	matted	calmed	placed	malice
59	MANAGEMENT		games	agent	magenta	meant	game
60	TIDEMARK		taker	dream	dimmer	marked	armed
61	ESTRANGE		gears	snare	grates	earns	groan

6

A music festival is being held in London. To get there, you would have to travel 12 km from Wiston. If you lived in Bridgeworth you would have to go 4 km further than from Wiston but 6 km less than from Hambury. From Fettle it is only half the distance to London that it would be from Hambury.

B 25

62 Which town is closest to London? _____

63 Which town is furthest from London? _____

64 How far is Bridgeworth from London? _____

65 How much further from London is Wiston than Fettle? _____

Now go to the Progress Chart to record your score! Total 65

Paper 2

Underline the two words in each line which are most similar in type or meaning.

Example   <u>dear</u> pleasant poor extravagant <u>expensive</u>

1 withdraw   build   retrain   construct   demolish

2 destroy   remove   put   place   lie

3 attempt   adjust   leave   reveal   try

4 starting   grave   thoughtful   ending   serious

5 easy   correct   wrong   complex   effortless

Underline the pair of words most opposite in meaning.

Example cup, mug   coffee, milk   <u>hot, cold</u>

6 flat, even   false, true   strange, wild

7 continuous, ended   allowed, admitted   flaky, dry

8 quick, swift   plain, elegant   hunch, guess

9 wet, damp   truth, honesty   criticise, praise

10 cured, improved   full, complete   well, ill

Underline the two words, one from each group, that go together to form a new word. The word in the first group always comes first.

Example (hand, <u>green</u>, for)   (light, <u>house</u>, sure)

11 (good, high, flat)   (friend, out, mate)

12 (cold, wet, at)   (put, tack, pie)

13 (for, try, down)   (lawn, late, sake)

14 (on, out, way)   (fold, cry, lie)

15 (left, in, far)   (vest, way, out)

Find the three-letter word which can be added to the letters in capitals to make a new word. The new word will complete the sentence sensibly.

B 22

Example   The cat sprang onto the MO.   <u>USE</u>

16–17 Jane's BHER told her that his cat had FOLED him to school that day. _____ _____

18–20 Her CLASSE told Seena she should TELEPH
her mother to come and collect her IMMEDILY.   _____ _____ _____

5

Find the four-letter word hidden at the end of one word and the beginning of the next word. The order of the letters may not be changed.

B 21

Example   The children had bats and balls.   <u>sand</u>

21 He reached the deadline in time.   _____

22 The rusty old door opened with a scary creak.   _____

23 Tara reminded her mother that Monday was a holiday.   _____

24 In winter the hen would stop laying eggs.   _____

25 The prisoner shouted his plea several times.   _____

5

Change the first word into the last word, by changing one letter at a time and making a new, different word in the middle.

B 13

Example   CASE   <u>CASH</u>   LASH

26 PUSH   _____   POST

27 REAR   _____   SEAT

28 LAST   _____   HOST

29 FINE   _____   MINT

30 STAR   _____   SNAG

5

Complete the following sentences by selecting the most sensible word from each group of words given in the brackets. Underline the words selected.

B 14

Example   The (<u>children</u>, books, foxes) carried the (houses, <u>books</u>, steps) home from the (greengrocer, <u>library</u>, factory).

31 When will we (land, address, arrive) in our (fresh, artistic, holiday) (conservatory, resort, canvas)?

32 Which (way, man, frog) do we (eat, go, hunt) to get to the (theatre, lunch, flower)?

33 The (quiet, hungry, learner) driver kept (eating, speeding, stalling) the car's (supper, engine, wheels).

34 In the (hungry, spotted, haunted) (bush, castle, wagon) lived an evil (spirit, brick, bathroom).

35 In (art, mathematics, history) we learn about (dance, football, graphs) and (television, numbers, drawing).

Choose two words, one from each set of brackets, to complete the sentences in the best way.

Example   Smile is to happiness as (drink, <u>tear</u>, shout) is to (whisper, laugh, <u>sorrow</u>).

36 Monday is to Wednesday as (Tuesday, Thursday, Sunday) is to (Monday, Wednesday, Saturday).

37 Flight is to aircraft as (walk, trial, sailing) is to (car, ship, automobile).

38 Rim is to plate as (picture, shore, water) is to (lake, painting, drink).

39 Uncertain is to sure as (tired, restricted, grateful) is to (late, unlimited, trained).

40 Trivial is to insignificant as (considerate, unstable, trembling) is to (generous, prudent, unkind).

Fill in the crosswords so that all the given words are included. You have been given one letter as a clue in each crossword.

41

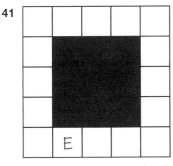

fried, hatch, death, fetch

42

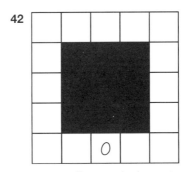

story, diary, grind, goats

43

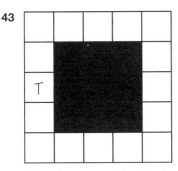

elect, brown, night, bathe

44

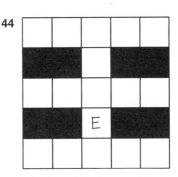

irate, after, forge, later

45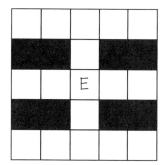

chest, metre, mocha, pleat

B 23

Give the missing numbers in the following sequences.

Example   2   4   6   8   <u>10</u>   <u>12</u>

46   62   58   ___   50   46   ___

47   7   9   12   ___   ___   27

48   1   5   3   ___   5   9   ___

49   25   20   30   ___   35   ___

50   2   4   8   ___   32   ___

B 24

If the code for BALLISTIC is < > ? ? £ % X £ +, what are the codes for the following words?

51 BALLS   _____

52 LIST   _____

53 STAB   _____

What do these codes stand for?

54 £ ? ?   _____

55 + > ? ?   _____

B 7

Underline the one word in each group which **cannot be made** from the letters of the word in capital letters.

Example   STATIONERY   stone   tyres   ration   <u>nation</u>   noisy

56 REMAINDER   mined   denim   rider   married   drained

57 WORKMANSHIP   shrimp   prism   hawks   plank   sharp

58 TELEVISION   version   invites   seven   event   list

59 ARRANGEMENT   remnant   manager   anger   garment   nearest

60 PERSONAL   snare   polar   salon   plain   loans

5

5

5

5

Anna supports France and England. Liam supports Wales and England. Malik does not support Scotland but supports Wales. Donna supports Scotland, England and Brazil. David hates football.

B 25

61 How many teams do Donna and Malik support together? _____

62 Which country has the most supporters? _____

2

Eleanor lives 5 km from school. Su lives nearest to school. Francesca lives 2 km closer than Eleanor, who lives 4 km further from the school than Su. Robert lives 1 km further than Su.

B 25

63 Who lives furthest from school? _____

64 How much nearer to school is Su than Francesca? _____

2

Charlotte is five years older than Lianne, who is four years younger than Lily. Lily is one year older than Ellie, who is three years older than Jessica. Ellie is 10.

B 25

65 Which two girls are twins? _____

1

Now go to the Progress Chart to record your score! **Total** **65**

Paper 3

Underline the word in the brackets closest in meaning to the words in capitals.

B 5

Example UNHAPPY (unkind death laughter <u>sad</u> friendly)

1 PULL, TUG (drop drag eat kick boat)

2 WASP, BEETLE (butterfly horse salmon snake mouse)

3 POMEGRANATE, TOMATO (sprout lettuce apple onion beetroot)

4 CONTRACT, PACT (agreement code shrink invitation signature)

5 WALES, FINLAND (London Essex Leeds Russia Kent)

5

Underline the two words, one from each group, which are the most opposite in meaning.

B 9

Example (dawn, <u>early</u>, wake) (<u>late</u>, stop, sunrise)

6 (wonder, love, try) (find, heat, hate)

7 (hard, fine, soft) (furry, effortless, light)

8 (reject, refill, waste) (conserve, rubbish, useful)

9 (fair, honest, closed) (just, truthful, dark)

10 (reduce, infinite, counted) (endless, hourly, limited)

5

Find the letter that will end the first word and start the second word.

B 10

Example   peac (h) ome

11 fus (___) dge

12 mat (___) lse

13 coa (___) imb

14 int (___) ath

15 shu (___) umb

5

Find a word that can be put in front of each of the following words to make new, compound words.

B 11

Example   cast   fall   ward   pour   *down*

16	knob	step	mat	bell	_____
17	by	still	point	pipe	_____
18	keeper	table	scale	share	_____
19	paper	agent	reel	flash	_____
20	ache	burn	beat	felt	_____

5

Find the four-letter word hidden at the end of one word and the beginning of the next word. The order of the letters may not be changed.

B 21

Example   The children had bats and balls.   *sand*

21 She is at her wits' end with her homework.   _____

22 Please empty your pockets before putting your trousers in the laundry.   _____

23 The tins are at the back of the cupboard.   _____

24 As it hurtled down the street, the car turned and spun round.   _____

25 The fiercest of dinosaurs lived throughout the cretaceous age.   _____

5

Find and underline the two words which need to change places for each sentence to make sense.

B 17

Example   She went to <u>letter</u> the <u>write</u>.

26 Who have could dreamed that it would come true?

27 After computer I like to play on my school.

28 Two plus four is two.

29 It is never steal to right.

30 Where in the China is world?

5

Give the missing numbers in the following sequences.

	Example	2	4	6	8	<u>10</u>	<u>12</u>
31	15	12	9	6		___	___
32	11	33	___	77	___	121	
33	128	64	32	___	8	___	
34	5	8	12	17	___	___	
35	54	45	36	___	18	___	

Fill in the crosswords so that all the given words are included. You have been given one letter as a clue in each crossword.

36

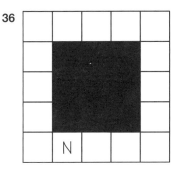

their, enter, paint, price

37

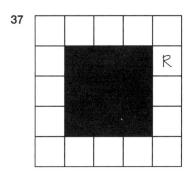

event, stand, shade, draft

38

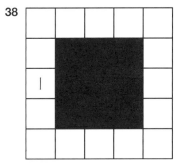

reign, thorn, faint, flair

39

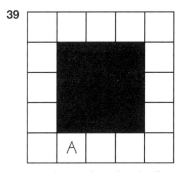

tardy, truth, taint, holly

40

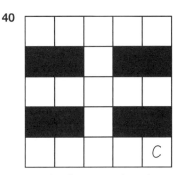

magic, flown, attic, ghost

Choose two words, one from each set of brackets, to complete the sentences in the best way.

B 15

Example Smile is to happiness as (drink, <u>tear</u>, shout) is to (whisper, laugh, <u>sorrow</u>).

41 First is to last as (late, second, aged) is to (fine, young, final).

42 Shirt is to cloth as (sock, shoe, earring) is to (string, grass, leather).

43 Past is to present as (once, lessen, increase) is to (multiply, last, first).

44 Halve is to double as (change, third, force) is to (remain, second, unravel).

45 Constant is to always as (final, unique, copied) is to (original, late, related).

5

If the code for C H A N G E A B L E is written ! ' £ $ % ^ £ & * ^, what are the codes for the following words?

B 24

46 HANG   _____

47 ABLE   _____

What do these codes stand for?

48 & £ * *   _____

49 & ^ £ $ _____

50 £ ! ' ^   _____

5

Underline the one word which **cannot be made** from the letters of the word in capital letters.

B 7

Example STATIONERY   stone   tyres   ration   <u>nation</u>   noisy

51 PORCELAIN	plain	clear	price	race	relay
52 COMMERCIAL	cream	realm	alert	moral	rice
53 GRINDSTONE	tried	stored	noted	rested	nesting
54 INVESTIGATE	tease	sting	ingest	testing	starve
55 SIGNATURE	agent	ignore	rents	great	surge

5

In football Alison can play in goal or in defence. Soraya can play in midfield or in attack. James never plays in goal, but can play in other positions. Lena can play in midfield or in attack. Kim can play in any position. Geeta can play in defence or midfield.

B 25

56 Who can play in any position except in goal?   _____

57 Which two children play the same positions?   _____

58 If Alison is ill, who will play in goal?   _____

59 How many children can play in attack? _____

60 How many children can play in midfield but not defence? _____

B 16

Rearrange the muddled letters in capitals to make a proper word. The answer will complete the sentence sensibly.

Example   A BEZAR is an animal with stripes.   <u>ZEBRA</u>

61 We put one foot in front of the other when we LWKA. _____

62 NALIF is another word for last. _____

63 We are taught a SENLOS. _____

64 I have TPSNE all my pocket money. _____

65 Twenty-six REELTTS make up the alphabet. _____

5

Now go to the Progress Chart to record your score!   **Total**   65

Paper 4

Underline the two words, one from each group, which are closest in meaning.

B 3

Example   (race, shop, <u>start</u>)   (finish, <u>begin</u>, end)

1 (push, trace, flash)   (take, shove, fly)

2 (weed, creep, weep)   (rush, cry, flip)

3 (spoil, try, mend)   (ignore, waste, repair)

4 (refuse, control, retry)   (manage, oppose, enjoy)

5 (uphold, agree, stay)   (refuse, support, change)

5

Find the three-letter word which can be added to the letters in capitals to make a new word. The new word will complete the sentence sensibly.

B 22

Example   The cat sprang onto the MO.   <u>USE</u>

6 We had chocolate PUDG for dessert. _____

7 It is a SE that it is raining, as we wanted to go out. _____

8 We had MALADE on our toast. _____

9 She decided to SPRLE marshmallows on her hot chocolate. _____

10 The store AGER asked the customers if she could help them. _____

5

Find the letter that will end the first word and start the second word.

B 10

Example peac (h) ome

11 mas (___) nit

12 sal (___) ach

13 tin (___) ard

14 pri (___) ask

15 man (___) dit

5

Find a word that can be put in front of each of the following words to make new, compound words.

B 11

Example cast fall ward pour _down_

16	doors	side	line	fit	_____
17	works	monger	clad	ware	_____
18	man	flake	drop	ball	_____
19	ball	lash	shadow	lid	_____
20	man	card	code	box	_____

5

Find the four-letter word hidden at the end of one word and the beginning of the next word. The order of the letters may not be changed.

B 21

Example The children had bats and balls. _sand_

21 Each inspector must be well trained. _____

22 The tired old man came along the street slowly. _____

23 The *Golden Pride* approached slowly along the track. _____

24 He had certainly made advances with his handwriting. _____

25 He applied for his library card because he liked reading. _____

5

Change the first word of the third pair in the same way as the other pairs to give a new word.

B 18

Example bind, hind bare, hare but, _hut_

26 pit, tip rat, tar tub, _____

27 made, mace fade, face ride, _____

28 part, start pale, stale peer, _____

29 seal, sale meal, male fear, _____

30 flea, leaf stag, tags plea, _____

5

Complete the following sentences by selecting the most sensible word from each group of words given in the brackets. Underline the words selected.

B 14

Example   The (<u>children</u>, books, foxes) carried the (houses, <u>books</u>, steps) home from the (greengrocer, <u>library</u>, factory).

31 The fastest (girl, cheetah, car) in the (shop, school, forest) came (last, once, first) in the 100 metre race.

32 I wonder if we will be (calling, eating, taking) a spelling (cry, test, man) next (cake, week, word).

33 (Charging, Flying, Climbing) mountains can be (trusting, easy, dangerous) in poor (weather, hunger, air).

34 Daisy (felt, wondered, knew) whether she should (try, fall, rub) to call for (food, excellence, assistance).

35 (Always, Never, Forever) forget to (start, make, brush) your (feet, hands, teeth) before going to bed.

5

Find and underline the two words which need to change places for each sentence to make sense.

B 17

Example   She went to <u>letter</u> the <u>write</u>.

36 Once upon a woman there lived an old time.

37 There been have two assemblies today.

38 The baby was crying the through all night.

39 This is the very last tell I am going to time you!

40 I wonder that he decided to do why.

5

Complete the following expressions by filling in the missing word.

B 15

Example   Pen is to ink as brush is to _paint_

41 Three is to third as nine is to _____ .

42 Spain is to Spanish as France is to _____ .

43 Month is to year as decade is to _____ .

44 High is to low as up is to _____ .

45 Land is to dry as sea is to _____ .

5

Give the two missing pairs of letters and numbers in the following sequences. The alphabet has been written out to help you.

B 23

A B C D E F G H I J K L M N O P Q R S T U V W X Y Z

Example   CQ   DP   EQ   FP   _GQ_   _HP_

46   C   F   I   L   __   __

47   DC   DD   DE   DF   __   __

48	A3	B5	C7	___	E11	___
49	YB	WD	___	SH	QJ	___
50	___	___	RQ	NM	JI	FE

5

Solve the problems by working out the letter codes. The alphabet has been written out to help you.

B 24

A B C D E F G H I J K L M N O P Q R S T U V W X Y Z

Example In a code SECOND is written as UGEQPF. How would you write THIRD? _VJKTF_

51 In a code PRINCE is written as NPGLAC. How would you write NICE? _____

52 In a code ICON is written as HBNM. What does SVHF stand for? _____

53 In a code APE is written as BRH. How would you write LOOK? _____

54 In a code FEEL is written as IHHO. How would you write WAIT? _____

55 In a code RICE is written as VMGI. How would you write DOG? _____

5

Ann and Rhinffrew like lemonade. Peter likes cola, but not lemonade. Siobhan likes orange and cola. Angus only likes cola.

B 25

56 Which is the most popular drink? _____

57 Which person likes the most types of drink? _____

2

Chester is west of Birmingham, but east of Bangor. Shrewsbury is south of Chester.

B 25

58 Which town is furthest west? _____

1

Three years ago Simeon was three years old. In four years' time he will be twice the age of his sister Sophie. Their mother is five times Simeon's age now. Their father is two years older than their mother.

B 25

59 How old will Sophie be in four years' time? _____

60 How old was their mother three years ago? _____

61 How old is their father now? _____

62 How much older is Simeon than Sophie? _____

4

If $a = 1$, $b = 3$, $c = 4$, $d = 6$, $e = 10$, find the answer to these calculations.

B 26

63 $e - d =$ _____

64 $d \div b =$ _____

65 $a + b + c =$ _____

3

Now go to the Progress Chart to record your score! **Total** **65**

16

1–5 Look at these groups of words.

H	C	G
Homes	Containers	Games

Choose the correct group for each of the words below. Write in the letter.

skipping ___   basket ___   Cluedo ___   urn ___

den ___   flat ___   cup ___   lodge ___

casket ___   snakes and ladders ___

B 1
5

Find the three-letter word which can be added to the letters in capitals to make a new word. The new word will complete the sentence sensibly.

B 22

Example   The cat sprang onto the MO.   <u>USE</u>

6 CARS are my favourite vegetables.

7 The nurse put some OINTT on the wound.

8 The WING machine was full of dirty clothes.

9 The old lady DEDED on her carer to help her get out of bed.

10 The volcano was INIVE and no longer spewed out molten lava.

5

Find the letter which will end the first word and start the second word.

B 10

Example   peac (<u>h</u>) ome

11 fin   (___) oze

12 mal   (___) ive

13 poin   (___) rip

14 kis   (___) ite

15 me   (___) age

5

Write the letters of each of the following words in alphabetical order, then circle the fifth letter in each word.

B 20

16 FAMILY   _____

17 READING   _____

18 LIGHTER   _____

19 TUESDAY   _____

20 BOUNCE   _____

5

Find the four-letter word hidden at the end of one word and the beginning of the next word. The order of the letters may not be changed.

    Example   The children had bats and balls.   _sand_

21 Sarah asked her brother to turn his music down.   _____

22 The teacher announced that there appeared to be
   a problem with the computers.   _____

23 The corporal ordered his troops to stand to attention.   _____

24 'Please stop interrupting!' said the teacher.   _____

25 The sofa remained in place by the door.   _____   **5**

Add one letter to the word in capital letters to make a new word. The meaning of the new word is given in the clue.

    Example   PLAN   simple   _plain_

26 EVER   not at all   _____

27 STRIP   a band of colour   _____

28 CHAP   not expensive   _____

29 THOUGH   in one side and out the other   _____

30 RESTED   taken by force   _____   **5**

Complete the following sentences by selecting the most sensible word from each group of words given in the brackets. Underline the words selected.

    Example   The (<u>children</u>, books, foxes) carried the (houses, <u>books</u>, steps) home
              from the (greengrocer, <u>library</u>, factory).

31 (Two, three, four) times (three, four, five) makes (eight, eighteen, eighty).

32 The (force, black, strong) wind blew through the (broken, pattern, fast) window.

33 In which (shirt, shop, shape) can we buy (card, painted, chocolate) (clouds, swimmers, cakes)?

34 Who (was, would, wish) like to (eat, hide, try) on their new school (uniform, canteen, hall)?

35 We were (shot, ate, flew) at by an (untidy, uneaten, unseen) (lunch, army, bedroom).   **5**

Complete the following sentences in the best way by choosing one word from each set of brackets.

    Example   Tall is to (tree, <u>short</u>, colour) as narrow is to (thin, white, <u>wide</u>).

36 Shout is to (whisper, scream, noisy) as loud is to (low, quiet, cosy).

37 Hat is to (face, head, coat) as mittens is to (cat, wool, hands).

38 Government is to (rule, elect, law) as school is to (teach, classroom, pupil).

39 Red is to (food, danger, colour) as centimetre is to (weight, green, measurement).

40 Grand is to (grown, impressive, lesson) as modest is to (reduced, proud, plain).

5

Fill in the crosswords so that all the given words are included. You have been given one letter as a clue in each crossword.

B 19

41

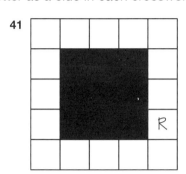

salad, daily, scale, entry

42

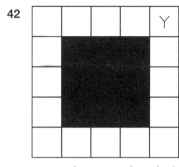

water, rings, yards, windy

43

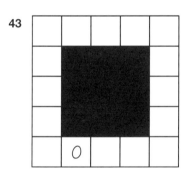

roads, elves, frame, fever

44

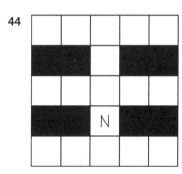

miser, sunny, funny, tryst

45

loves, caves, halls, misty

5

If the code for TRAVEL is USBWFM, what are the codes for the following words?

B 24

46 LEVEL _____

47 LEAVE _____

48 EVER _____

3

If the code for CUTE is DVUF, what do these codes stand for?

B 24

49 SBSF _____

50 MJTU _____

2

If a = 3, b = 5, c = 12, d = 15, e = 2, f = 10, give the answers to these calculations as letters.

B 26

51 d − f = _____

52 a + e = _____

53 b × a = _____

54 d ÷ a = _____

55 b × e = _____

5

Choose the word or phrase that makes each sentence true.

B 14

Example A LIBRARY always has (posters, a carpet, <u>books</u>, DVDs, stairs).

56 A DESK always has (glass, books, pens, legs, children).

57 A LAKE is always (sandy, wet, salty, blue, deep).

58 A TRUCK always has (a steering wheel, four seats, passengers, petrol, carpet).

59 A COUNTRY always has (a king, a queen, a parliament, a border, a president).

60 GLASS is always (hard, transparent, clean, square, frosted).

5

B 25

Peter and Ruth Jones

David Jones and Joan Thomas   Jessica Jones and Mark Stevens

Molly Jones   Olivia Stevens

61 Peter is David's (brother, uncle, father, grandfather).

62 Jessica is Ruth's (sister, aunt, mother, daughter).

63 Molly is Ruth's (daughter, sister, mother, granddaughter).

64 Olivia is David's (daughter, niece, mother, sister).

65 Peter is Mark's (father, brother, grandfather, father-in-law).

5

Now go to the Progress Chart to record your score!   Total 65

20

Paper 6

Underline the pair of words most similar in meaning.

    Example come, go   <u>roams, wanders</u>   fear, fare

1 awake, asleep   gift, present   sweet, bitter

2 top, peak   warm, cool   hole, hill

3 big, small   question, answer   follow, pursue

4 please, delight   create, destroy   fall, rise

5 failure, victory   judgement, decision allow, refuse

Find the three-letter word which can be added to the letters in capitals to make a new word. The new word will complete the sentence sensibly.

Example   The cat sprang onto the MO. <u>USE</u>

6 He found it difficult to SK as his mouth was so dry.   _____

7 You must MULLY three by three to get 9.   _____

8 SE birthday is it today?   _____

9 She found the question difficult to UNDERSD.   _____

10 The sisters had a DISAGREET over who should
     get the bed near the window.   _____

Find the letter which will end the first word and start the second word.

    Example peac (<u>h</u>) ome

11 fligh (__) rip

12 pra   (__) onder

13 flak (__) nd

14 ris   (__) ite

15 bea (__) rial

Rearrange the muddled letters in capitals to make a proper word. The answer will complete the sentence sensibly.

    Example A BEZAR is an animal with stripes.   <u>ZEBRA</u>

16 The time is now a ATEQRRU past five.   _____

17 He had VESRREED the car into the parking space.   _____

18 I like to have some RVYAG on my mashed potatoes. _____

19 The manager named the SRELPAY for the next match. _____

20 In the drought, we were all asked to NCVROSEE water. _____

5

Find the four-letter word hidden at the end of one word and the beginning of the next word. The order of the letters may not be changed.

B 21

    Example   The children had bats and balls.   *sand*

21 The Vikings fled overland before regrouping. _____

22 Many frozen icecaps are found north of Canada. _____

23 Each term my school tests the fire alarm to make sure it is working. _____

24 Kevin ended the conversation fairly quickly. _____

25 Tom's biggest problem was the neighbours playing loud music. _____

5

Change the first word of the third pair in the same way as the other pairs to give a new word.

B 18

    Example   bind, hind   bare, hare   but, *hut*

26 race, rate   face, fate   place, _____

27 can, cane   trip, tripe   prim, _____

28 port, sort   pane, sane   page, _____

29 stark, shark   stone, shone   stock, _____

30 file, life   pole, lope   ride, _____

5

Find and underline the two words which need to change places for each sentence to make sense.

B 17

    Example   She went to <u>letter</u> the <u>write</u>.

31 When go you like to would to the zoo?

32 Nature is an amazing wonder of flying.

33 Island is an Britain nation in the continent of Europe.

34 I am planning to deposit fifty bank in the pounds.

35 Gabriel found that the heat about questions were extremely difficult to do.

5

Choose two words, one from each set of brackets, to complete the sentences in the best way.

B 15

    Example   Tall is to (tree, <u>short</u>, colour) as narrow is to (thin, white, <u>wide</u>).

36 Sugar is to (grain, sweet, bitter) as lemon is to (lime, drink, sour).

37 True is to (argument, lie, truth) as vain is to (calm, preen, vanity).

38 Salad is to (can, fork, vegetables) as trifle is to (eat, pie, fruit).

39 Tooth is to (foot, mouth, clean) as brain is to (skull, nerves, blood).

40 Still is to (calm, active, fizzy) as movement is to (fast, motion, bubbly).

Fill in the crosswords so that all the given words are included. You have been given one letter as a clue in each crossword.

41

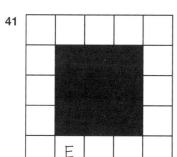

small, revel, tails, taper

42

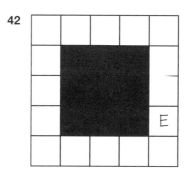

trays, place, paint, edges

43

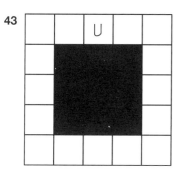

thick, falls, stick, fount

44

feeds, bride, taste, ideas

45

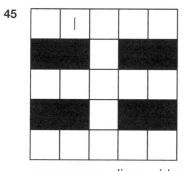

cures, moves, diver, wider

Rearrange the letters in capitals to make another word. The new word has something to do with the first two words or phrases.

    Example   spot   soil   SAINT   <u>STAIN</u>

46 final   end   SALT   _____

47 prickle   bush   NORTH   _____

48	story	yarn	LATE	_____
49	rotten	not fresh	LEAST	_____
50	servant	hard worker	VALES	_____

If a = 10, b = 2, c = 3, d = 7, e = 5, give the answers to these calculations as letters.

51 b + c + e = _____

52 be = _____

53 a − e = _____

54 (d − b) × b = _____

55 a ÷ b = _____

Change one word so that the sentence makes sense. Underline the word you are taking out and write your new word on the line.

Example   I waited in line to buy a <u>book</u> to see the film.   *ticket*

56   The train for Birmingham left the port on time.   _____

57   During the freezing summer months, snow fell almost daily.   _____

58   The teacher examined his patient with a stethoscope.   _____

59   Queen Victoria reigned for many days in the nineteenth century.   _____

60   The florist sold loaves, rolls and a selection of cakes.   _____

Rajeev buys three magazines every week. He likes magazines about pop music, computer games and television. Carl hates football, but buys a pop music magazine. Gill buys pop music and fashion magazines. Saskia does not buy any magazines.

61   Which is the most popular magazine?   _____

62   How many children buy computer game magazines?   _____

Jan, Cilla, Vijay and Finn are friends. Finn and Vijay like gymnastics. The other children like hockey. Jan and Finn like tennis. Cilla's favourite is hockey, but she hates gymnastics. All but Finn like swimming.

63   Which is the most popular sport?   _____

64   Who likes gymnastics and swimming?   _____

65   Who likes three sports?   _____

Paper 7

Underline the word in the brackets closest in meaning to the word in capitals.

B 5

Example UNHAPPY (unkind   death   laughter   <u>sad</u>   friendly)

1 TRACK   (music   frame   scale   path   bed)

2 FRAIL   (weak   lively   success   timely   true)

3 SOFA   (table   settee   television   bunk   pillow)

4 ANTIQUE   (tasty   ornament   fresh   steady   old)

5 DOMESTICATED   (famous   wild   tamed   hunted   criminal)

5

Underline the pair of words most opposite in meaning.

B 9

Example   cup, mug   coffee, milk   <u>hot, cold</u>

6 spend, save   dye, colour   fall, drop

7 fly, float   advance, retreat   clue, hint

8 soak, wet   open, full   reckless, careful

9 flexible, rigid   gentle, soft   damp, moist

10 build, support   wind, crank   clutter, order

5

Find the letter which will end the first word and start the second word.

B 10

Example   peac (<u>h</u>) ome

11 fla   (__) ongue

12 mirro (__) ain

13 cak   (__) nter

14 ove   (__) ew

15 fur   (__) ield

5

Find a word that can be put in front of each of the following words to make new, compound words.

B 11

Example   cast   fall   ward   pour   *down*

16 hill   stairs   set   keep   _____

17 fall   shirt   mare   club   _____

18	mill	fall	melon	proof	_____
19	house	post	keeper	way	_____
20	stop	way	frame	man	_____

B 21

Find the four-letter word hidden at the end of one word and the beginning of the next word. The order of the letters may not be changed.

Example   The children had bats and balls.   *sand*

21 Please replace that book on the shelf later.   _____

22 That ornament would be extremely valuable if it were not damaged.   _____

23 People of my age are often asked to give advice on living a long life.   _____

24 The spies watched the suspects through binoculars.   _____

25 It is clear that the sack needed some urgent repair.   _____

B 13

Change the first word into the last word, by changing one letter at a time and making a new, different word in the middle.

Example   CASE   *CASH*   LASH

26 FAST   _____   FACE

27 FINE   _____   FARE

28 TRAY   _____   TRIP

29 FLEW   _____   CLAW

30 BEST   _____   BEAR

B 14

Complete the following sentences by selecting the most sensible word from each group of words given in the brackets. Underline the words selected.

Example   The (children, books, foxes) carried the (houses, books, steps) home from the greengrocer, library, factory).

31 The (cow, bird, girl) sat on its (nest, chair, floor), looking after its (chicks, cubs, hands).

32 The (lazy, late, first) man on the (river, moon, sun) wore a special (spacesuit, oar, cane).

33 The (pink, young, brown) leaves fell off the (cat, trees, sky) in (autumn, spring, grass).

34 A (rabbit, friend, doctor) has to (eat, march, train) for many (meals, lungs, years).

35 The fast moving (man, river, beaver) flowed (quickly, hungrily, lazily) to the (sky, race, sea).

Find and underline the two words which need to change places for each sentence to make sense.

Example She went to <u>letter</u> the <u>write</u>.

36 You should never full with your mouth speak.

37 Can't have each we a banana?

38 Health is good for your swimming.

39 It was a very pretty day on the warm beach.

40 The old car got into his battered man.

5

Complete the following expressions by filling in the missing word.

Example Pen is to ink as brush is to *paint*

41 Box is to lid as house is to _____ .

42 Love is to hate as laugh is to _____ .

43 Tall is to taller as cool is to _____ .

44 Wales is to Welsh as Spain is to _____ .

45 Scarf is to neck as glove is to _____ .

5

Fill in the crosswords so that all the given words are included. You have been given one letter as a clue in each crossword.

46

O

house, state, match, maids

47

R

fight, flake, tiger, error

48

O

haunt, right, river, roach

49

A

sites, plait, aspen, avail

50

dress, trees, cider, tasty

5

If a = 2, b = 4, c = 6, d = 8 and e = 12, find the value of the following calculations.

B 26

51 e + b = _____

52 e − a = _____

53 a × b = _____

54 (e − d) + c = _____

55 $\dfrac{d}{b}$ = _____

5

Rearrange the letters in capitals to make another word. The new word has something to do with the first two words.

B 16

Examples spot soil   SAINT <u>STAIN</u>

56 javelin   point   REAPS   _____

57 begin   commence   TARTS   _____

58 tassle   edge   FINGER   _____

59 quiet   hushed   LISTEN   _____

60 support love   RACE   _____

5

Choose the word or phrase that makes each sentence true.

B 14

Example   A LIBRARY always has (posters, a carpet, <u>books</u>, DVDs, stairs).

61 A SHOP always has (carpets, goods, dresses, women, stairs).

62 A BANK always has (customers, men, pictures, mirrors, money).

63 A PARTY always has (music, food, balloons, guests, gifts).

64 A GARDEN always has (flowers, a bench, trees, earth, a swing).

65 A FLORIST always has (balloons, toys, flowers, chocolates, trees).

5

Now go to the Progress Chart to record your score!   Total   65

Paper 1

1 test, exam
2 rot, decay
3 eat, consume
4 light, pale
5 extend, enlarge
6 then, now
7 large, tiny
8 loose, tight
9 hollow, solid
10 first, final
11 teacher, children, lunches
12 try, swimming, tide
13 cows, huddled, field
14 team, goal, match
15 whisked, dessert, fork
16 SHADES, DASHES
17 TEARS, RATES
18 PEARS, SPEAR
19 FLESH, SHELF
20 STEAL, LEAST
21 tear
22 carp
23 loan
24 moon
25 calm
26 e
27 t
28 m
29 r
30 p
31 lake, boat
32 you, I
33 mechanic, car
34 is, do
35 caged, angry
36 TU
37 XV
38 NO
39 Z11
40 CE
41 b
42 s
43 m
44 y
45 a

46
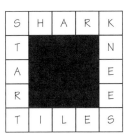

S	H	A	R	K
T				N
A				E
R				E
T	I	L	E	S

47

F	R	O	N	T
R				R
E				I
S				E
H	E	A	D	S

48

A	B	O	V	E
L				L
O				V
F				E
T	U	F	T	S

49

R	U	P	E	E
O				M
U				P
N				T
D	A	I	S	Y

50

G	R	U	E	L
R				A
A				U
N				G
D	O	U	G	H

51 * − : &
52 $ − : *
53 & − : £ −
54 TAR
55 TAINT
56 tamed
57 every
58 matted
59 games
60 dimmer
61 groan
62 Fettle
63 Hambury
64 16 km
65 1 km

Paper 2

1 build, construct
2 put, place
3 attempt, try
4 grave, serious
5 easy, effortless
6 false, true

7 continuous, ended
8 plain, elegant
9 criticise, praise
10 well, ill
11 flatmate
12 attack
13 forsake
14 outcry
15 invest
16 ROT
17 LOW
18 MAT
19 ONE
20 ATE
21 here
22 rope
23 rare
24 play
25 ease
26 POSH
27 SEAR
28 LOST
29 MINE
30 STAG
31 arrive, holiday, resort
32 way, go, theatre
33 learner, stalling, engine
34 haunted, castle, spirit
35 mathematics, graphs, numbers
36 Thursday, Saturday
37 sailing, ship
38 shore, lake
39 restricted, unlimited
40 considerate, generous

41

F	E	T	C	H
R				A
I				T
E				C
D	E	A	T	H

42

G	R	I	N	D
O				I
A				A
T				R
S	T	O	R	Y

43

B	R	O	W	N
A				I
T				G
H				H
E	L	E	C	T

44

I	R	A	T	E
	F			
L	A	T	E	R
	E			
F	O	R	G	E

45

M	O	C	H	A
	H			
P	L	E	A	T
	S			
M	E	T	R	E

46 54, 42
47 16, 21
48 7, 7
49 25, 30
50 16, 64
51 < > ? ? %
52 ? £ % X
53 % X > <
54 ILL
55 CALL
56 drained
57 plank
58 version
59 nearest
60 plain
61 4
62 England
63 Eleanor
64 2 km
65 Jessica and Lianne

Paper 3

1 drag
2 butterfly
3 apple
4 agreement
5 Russia
6 love, hate
7 hard, effortless
8 waste, conserve
9 fair, dark
10 infinite, limited
11 e
12 e
13 l
14 o
15 n
16 door
17 stand
18 time
19 news
20 heart

21 send
22 seem
23 area
24 cart
25 sage
26 have, could
27 computer, school
28 four, two
29 steal, right
30 China, world
31 3, 0
32 55, 99
33 16, 4
34 23, 30
35 27, 9

36

P	A	I	N	T
R				H
I				E
C				I
E	N	T	E	R

37

S	T	A	N	D
H				R
A				A
D				F
E	V	E	N	T

38

F	L	A	I	R
A				E
I				I
N				G
T	H	O	R	N

39

T	R	U	T	H
A				O
I				L
N				L
T	A	R	D	Y

40

M	A	G	I	C
		H		
F	L	O	W	N
		S		
A	T	T	I	C

41 aged, young
42 shoe, leather
43 lessen, multiply
44 change, remain
45 unique, original
46 ' £ $ %
47 £ & * ^
48 BALL
49 BEAN
50 ACHE
51 relay
52 alert
53 rested
54 starve
55 ignore
56 James
57 Soraya, Lena
58 Kim
59 4
60 2
61 WALK
62 FINAL
63 LESSON
64 SPENT
65 LETTERS

Paper 4

1 push, shove
2 weep, cry
3 mend, repair
4 control, manage
5 uphold, support
6 DIN
7 HAM
8 ARM
9 INK
10 MAN
11 k
12 e
13 y
14 m
15 e
16 out
17 iron
18 snow
19 eye
20 post
21 chin
22 meal
23 idea
24 dead
25 heap
26 but
27 rice
28 steer
29 fare
30 leap
31 girl, school, first
32 taking, test, week
33 climbing, dangerous, weather
34 wondered, try, assistance

35 never, brush, teeth
36 woman, time
37 been, have
38 the, all
39 tell, time
40 that, why
41 ninth
42 French
43 century
44 down
45 wet
46 O, R
47 DG, DH
48 D9, F13
49 UF, OL
50 ZY, VU
51 LGAC
52 TWIG
53 MQRO
54 ZDLW
55 HSK
56 cola
57 Siobhan
58 Bangor
59 5
60 27
61 32
62 5 years
63 4
64 2
65 8

Paper 5

1–5 Give one mark for each two correct answers: skipping G, basket C, Cluedo G, urn C, den H, flat H, cup C, lodge H, casket C, snakes and ladders G.

6 ROT
7 MEN
8 ASH
9 PEN
10 ACT
11 d
12 l
13 t
14 s
15 w
16 Ⓜ
17 Ⓘ
18 Ⓛ
19 Ⓣ
20 Ⓞ
21 herb
22 reap
23 lord
24 pint
25 fare
26 never
27 stripe
28 cheap
29 through

30 wrested
31 two, four, eight
32 strong, broken
33 shop, chocolate, cakes
34 would, try, uniform
35 shot, unseen, army
36 whisper, quiet
37 head, hands
38 rule, teach
39 colour, measurement
40 impressive, plain

41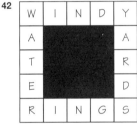

42

43

44

45

46 MFWFM
47 MFBWF
48 FWFS

49 RARE
50 LIST
51 b
52 b
53 d
54 b
55 f
56 legs
57 wet
58 a steering wheel
59 a border
60 hard
61 father
62 daughter
63 granddaughter
04 niece
65 father-in-law

Paper 6

1 gift, present
2 top, peak
3 follow, pursue
4 please, delight
5 judgement, decision
6 PEA
7 TIP
8 WHO
9 TAN
10 MEN
11 t
12 y
13 e
14 k
15 t
16 QUARTER
17 REVERSED
18 GRAVY
19 PLAYERS
20 CONSERVE
21 dove
22 nice
23 real
24 vine
25 then
26 plate
27 prime
28 sage
29 shock
30 dire
31 go, would
32 Nature, flying
33 Island, Britain
34 bank, pounds
35 heat, questions
36 sweet, sour
37 truth, vanity
38 vegetables, fruit
39 mouth, skull
40 calm, motion

Bond Verbal Reasoning Assessment Papers 9–10 years Book 2

41

```
T A I L S
A ■ ■ ■ M
P ■ ■ ■ A
E ■ ■ ■ L
R E V E L
```

42

```
P L A C E
A ■ ■ ■ D
I ■ ■ ■ G
N ■ ■ ■ E
T R A Y S
```

43

```
F O U N T
A ■ ■ ■ H
L ■ ■ ■ I
L ■ ■ ■ C
S T I C K
```

44

```
B R I D E
■ ■ D ■ ■
F E E D S
■ ■ A ■ ■
T A S T E
```

45

```
W I D E R
■ ■ I ■ ■
M O V E S
■ ■ E ■ ■
C U R E S
```

46 LAST
47 THORN
48 TALE
49 STALE
50 SLAVE
51 a
52 a
53 e
54 a
55 e
56 <u>port</u>, station
57 <u>summer</u>, winter
58 <u>teacher</u>, doctor
59 <u>days</u>, years
60 <u>florist</u>, baker
61 pop music
62 1
63 swimming
64 Vijay
65 Jan

Paper 7

1 path
2 weak
3 settee
4 old
5 tamed
6 spend, save
7 advance, retreat
8 reckless, careful
9 flexible, rigid
10 clutter, order
11 t
12 r
13 e
14 n
15 y
16 up
17 night
18 water
19 gate
20 door
21 flat
22 torn
23 gear
24 swat
25 knee
26 FACT
27 FIRE
28 TRAP
29 FLAW
30 BEAT
31 bird, nest, chicks
32 first, moon, spacesuit
33 brown, trees, autumn
34 doctor, train, years
35 river, quickly, sea
36 full, speak
37 have, we
38 health, swimming
39 pretty, warm
40 car, man
41 roof
42 cry
43 cooler
44 Spanish
45 hand

46

```
M A I D S
A ■ ■ ■ T
T ■ ■ ■ A
C ■ ■ ■ T
H O U S E
```

47

```
F L A K E
I ■ ■ ■ R
G ■ ■ ■ R
H ■ ■ ■ O
T I G E R
```

48

```
R O A C H
I ■ ■ ■ A
V ■ ■ ■ U
E ■ ■ ■ N
R I G H T
```

49

```
A S P E N
■ ■ L ■ ■
A V A I L
■ ■ I ■ ■
S I T E S
```

50

```
C I D E R
■ ■ R ■ ■
T R E E S
■ ■ S ■ ■
T A S T Y
```

51 16
52 10
53 8
54 10
55 2
56 SPEAR
57 START
58 FRINGE
59 SILENT
60 CARE
61 goods
62 money
63 guests

64 earth
65 flowers

Paper 8

1–5 *Give one mark for each two correct answers:* noun B, monitor C, verb B, violin A, disk drive C, mouse C, guitar A, preposition B, piano A, flute A.

6 pull, push
7 wild, tame
8 shut, open
9 combine, separate
10 friend, enemy
11 s
12 y
13 l
14 t
15 l
16 takeaway
17 update
18 blameless
19 office
20 peanut
21 wasp
22 bush
23 thin
24 seat
25 army
26 RICE
27 MEAT
28 PLAY
29 FLAT
30 BEAR
31 O15
32 YW
33 FI
34 PD
35 MO

36

T	R	U	S	T
A	■	■	■	H
M	■	■	■	O
E	■	■	■	S
S	H	O	V	E

37

P	R	I	Z	E
R	■	■	■	V
E	■	■	■	E
S	■	■	■	R
S	U	N	N	Y

38

I	C	I	N	G
N	■	■	■	R
P	■	■	■	A
U	■	■	■	V
T	A	N	G	Y

39

U	L	T	R	A
■	■	Y	■	■
H	A	P	P	Y
■	■	E	■	■
H	A	S	T	Y

40

F	U	N	N	Y
■	■	I	■	■
R	I	G	H	T
■	■	H	■	■
T	I	T	L	E

41 sort
42 play
43 fly
44 stab
45 kid
46 TIE
47 MAT
48 RED
49 LEAP
50 TALE
51 blue team
52 15
53 10
54 Tuesday
55 14
56 e
57 b
58 c
59 f
60 b
61 EGILMNT
62 T
63 G
64 ARSTY
65 S

Paper 9

1 bread
2 right
3 bold
4 scream
5 amazed
6 sad

7 raise
8 arrive
9 exclude
10 join
11 RUM
12 RAN
13 OWN
14 ARM
15 TEA
16 undertake
17 upright
18 throughout
19 downstairs
20 cupboard
21 then
22 bite
23 send
24 pout
25 mask
26 fit, flame
27 word, tolls
28 mile, self
29 able, scarf
30 rob, event
31 goalkeeper, save, match
32 eat, vegetables, good
33 old, walk, stick
34 dress, modern, belt
35 time, ancient, witch
36 huge, short
37 early, excited
38 crowded, bare
39 fasten, twist
40 rest, stay

41

Q	U	I	L	L
U	■	■	■	A
E	■	■	■	R
E	■	■	■	G
R	A	N	G	E

42

F	L	O	O	R
R	■	■	■	H
I	■	■	■	Y
E	■	■	■	M
D	R	A	P	E

43

C	R	E	P	E
H	■	■	■	R
E	■	■	■	A
E	■	■	■	S
R	I	F	L	E

44

G	R	A	V	E
	F			
M	I	T	R	E
			E	
F	I	R	E	S

45

B	I	T	E	S
		R		
T	H	A	N	K
		P		
T	A	S	T	E

46 PK, PM
47 M, S
48 Q9, O11
49 OJ, RH
50 KM, PH
51 7325
52 5237
53 5247
54 1352
55 1852
56 ACJKOPST
57 T
58 K
59 CNORTUY
60 T
61 Jem
62 10
63 English
64 German
65 Italian

Paper 10

1 sponge, ship
2 twig, nest
3 heart, friend
4 next, future
5 undecided, complicated
6 INK
7 TEN
8 PAR
9 LIT
10 OUR
11 rot
12 dice
13 deal
14 bear
15 treat
16 bare

17 torn
18 fear
19 hall
20 arch
21 late, cramp
22 prim, gape
23 tile, sight
24 stand, brought
25 mine, clay
26 lunch
27 sly
28 knock
29 poke
30 green
31 horse, hay, stable
32 night, hooting, distance
33 road, ways, traffic
34 teacher, pupils, homework
35 girls, mother, cinema
36 outside, rainy
37 year, day
38 month, first
39 lunch, lasagne
40 mother, baby
41 LN
42 S19
43 OP
44 WU
45 TV
46 quick, slow
47 save, spend
48 attack, retreat
49 near, distant
50 specific, general
51–55 citsilaer, taerter, tcane, tcarter, tsomla
56 612
57 9123
58 9136
59 SURE
60 HUES
61 toffee and fudge
62 chocolate and sweets
63 Eric
64 Ann
65 Farook

Paper 11

1 cheerful, happy
2 disappear, vanish
3 flash, flare
4 career, profession
5 pay, salary
6 ROW
7 RAW
8 KIN
9 SIT

10 tar
11 house
12 sea
13 down
14 back
15 watch
16 hate
17 ants
18 sour
19 slay
20 rope
21 GALE
22 POST OR PART
23 BEST
24 CREW
25 SPAR
26 radio, music
27 reach, managed
28 month, day
29 hunting, lions
30 queue, wait

31

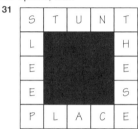

S	T	U	N	T
L				H
E				E
E				S
P	L	A	C	E

32

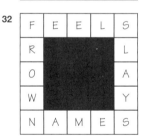

F	E	E	L	S
R				L
O				A
W				Y
N	A	M	E	S

33

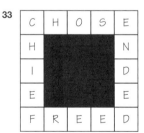

C	H	O	S	E
H				N
I				D
E				E
F	R	E	E	D

34

S	E	V	E	N
		E		
P	R	I	S	M
		L		
H	A	S	T	E

35

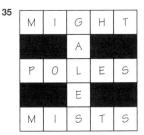

M	I	G	H	T
		A		
P	O	L	E	S
		E		
M	I	S	T	S

36 AK, AM
37 OS, RV
38 LI, NK
39 DQ, DO
40 IP, H3
41 ♦ ○ ● ♥
42 & ♥ ♦ ○ ●
43 ○ ● ♥ ♦ ▲
44 HEAR
45 RATE
46–47 Eagles eat mice. Eagles are predators
48–49 Spain is hot. Palm trees never grow in cold countries.
50–51 Earth is further from the Sun than Venus. Venus is hotter than Earth.
52 *Eastenders*
53 Joaquin
54 Molly
55 Rashid and Tom
56 t
57 q
58 s
59 r
60 u
61 PCKN
62 QDRS
63 GOOD
64 BSX
65 QLRDE

Paper 12

1 smart, fast
2 body, smile
3 mud, sand
4 desert, ocean
5 field, meadow
6 PEN
7 PIP
8 ADD
9 EAR
10 APE
11 y
12 r
13 t
14 r
15 l
16 netball
17 flatmate
18 pattern

19 goodwill
20 manage
21 hiss
22 mane
23 pear
24 tilt
25 vein
26 self, shell
27 brow, shone
28 hare, smash
29 rate, pact
30 last, tone
31 trees, leaves
32 race, first
33 bowl, breakfast
34 silver, gold
35 find, dig
36 HX
37 QN
38 WM
39 WD
40 JQ
41 3491
42 3428
43 3528
44 2849
45 2528
46 Li
47 cat and dog
48 Sharif
49 2
50 5
51 h
52 h
53 f
54 d
55 h
56 flower, petrol
57 garage, vet
58 moon's, sun's
59 foot, neck
60 marshmallow, cream
61 UDWHV
62 RNWO
63 SALE
64 SHOW
65 PDVN

Paper 13

1 B
2 D
3 C
4 A
5 B
6 hunt, search
7 similar, alike
8 overtake, pass
9 show, display
10 vague, unclear
11 pass
12 conflict

13 damage
14 follow
15 doubtful
16 can
17 light
18 hit
19 bright
20 smart
21 green
22 wood
23 fire
24 hand
25 hair
26 sand
27 lace
28 torn
29 term
30 fort
31 man
32 sore
33 plot
34 hop
35 rip
36 bake, oven
37 Bindy, Annabel
38 homework, fingers
39 red, wild
40 red, read
41 e
42 h
43 r
44 t
45 k
46 3115
47 8277
48 2751
49 5117
50 3297
51 David
52 Peter
53 16
54 23
55 Town D
56 PAIRS
57 EXITS
58 SAUCE
59 SAGE
60 DANGER
61 butcher, baker
62 tame, wild
63 hole, nest
64 Sunday, December
65 nurse, teacher

Paper 14

1 swift, fast
2 back, rear
3 miniature, small
4 aim, goal
5 pole, rod

Bond Verbal Reasoning Assessment Papers 9–10 years Book 2

ANSWERS

6 brilliant, dull
7 rude, polite
8 rise, fall
9 criticise, praise
10 relaxed, tense
11 plain
12 grace
13 pack
14 grain
15 star
16 e
17 t
18 d
19 k
20 p
21 hole
22 edge
23 cane
24 this
25 rind
26 PART
27 MIST
28 SOAR
29 BRAT
30 CUTS
31 TEST
32 ALSO
33 PEAR
34 PINT
35 RARE
36 r
37 e
38 t
39 t
40 b
41 pound, beat
42 lower, reduce
43 injure, damage
44 sickness, illness
45 tough, strong
46 war
47 water
48 weather

49 pass
50 back
51 QN, UN
52 CC, XX
53 RP, PN
54 PO, PQ
55 I5, K6
56 PEAR
57 CLAP
58 PALE
59 LEER
60 PALACE
61 wake, sleep
62 notes, strings
63 alive, dead
64 moon, sun
65 hungry, full

Paper 15

1 ask, request
2 shiny, glistening
3 destroyed, broken
4 cross, angry
5 drum, tap
6 shy, confident
7 cause, effect
8 light, heavy
9 tired, energetic
10 rare, common
11 r
12 b
13 l
14 r
15 y
16 lone
17 shun
18 cast
19 itch
20 heat
21 b
22 c

23 t
24 f
25 w
26 dragon
27 cove
28 ration
29 shin
30 meter
31 track, train
32 England, Kent
33 films, music
34 home, late
35 house, newspaper
36 slow, high
37 overlook, honour
38 water, coal
39 wet, cold
40 bird, mammal
41 10
42 45
43 E
44 E
45 D
46 m
47 y
48 e
49 d
50 l
51 LEAP
52 FALSE
53 WEAK
54 ANGERS
55 MELON
56 PAST
57 MACE or MITE
58 ARMS
59 SNIP
60 FLAW
61 EO
62 WW
63 ST
64 ZV
65 Z26

Paper 8

Look at these groups of words.

B 1

	A	B	C
	Musical instruments	Parts of speech	Computer terms

1–5 Choose the correct group for each of the words below. Write in the letter.

noun ___   monitor ___   verb ___   violin ___   disk drive ___

mouse ___   guitar ___   preposition ___   piano ___   flute ___

5

Underline the pair of words most opposite in meaning.

B 9

Example   cup, mug   coffee, milk   <u>hot, cold</u>

6 start, begin   pull, push   fight, battle

7 wild, tame   medium, middle   stale, old

8 shut, open   tight, cramped   fix, mend

9 try, attempt   combine, separate   stay, remain

10 filter, flow   friend, enemy   bump, knock

5

Find the letter that will end the first word and start the second word.

B 10

Example   peac (<u>h</u>) ome

11 dres (___) ign

12 pla (___) oke

13 shal (___) ove

14 trai (___) iara

15 dril (___) ong

5

Underline the two words, one from each group, that go together to form a new word. The word in the first group always comes first.

B 8

Example   (hand, <u>green</u>, for)   (light, <u>house</u>, sure)

16 (take, bring, seat)   (home, away, back)

17 (up, in, at)   (day, week, date)

18 (hunt, weak, blame)   (on, less, full)

19 (on, off, down)   (rest, step, ice)

20 (snap, pea, spice)   (nut, bag, hot)

5

Find the four-letter word hidden at the end of one word and the beginning of the next word. The order of the letters may not be changed.

B 21

Example   The children had bats and balls.   <u>sand</u>

21 Joe was pleased he didn't have any homework that night.   _____

22 He was surprised when the bus halted at the stop.   _____

23 Janine felt proud of herself for finishing fourth in the race.   _____

24 Apples eaten quickly will give you indigestion.   _____

25 The car my brother just bought is bright red.   _____

5

Change the first word into the last word, by changing one letter at a time and making a new, different word in the middle.

B 13

Example   CASE   <u>CASH</u>   LASH

26 NICE   _____   RACE

27 SEAT   _____   MOAT

28 PLAN   _____   SLAY

29 FEAT   _____   FLAY

30 BEAN   _____   TEAR

5

Fill in the missing letters and numbers. The alphabet has been written out to help you.

B 23

A B C D E F G H I J K L M N O P Q R S T U V W X Y Z

Example   AB is to CD as PQ is to <u>RS</u>.

31 C3 is to E5 as M13 is to _____.

32 WU is to TR as BZ is to _____.

33 HK is to MP as AD is to _____.

34 RR is to XL as JJ is to _____.

35 AC is to EG as IK is to _____.

5

Fill in the crosswords so that all the given words are included. You have been given one letter as a clue in each crossword.

B 19

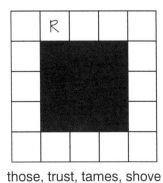

36

those, trust, tames, shove

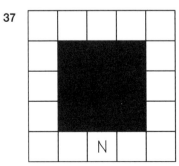

37

press, prize, every, sunny

38

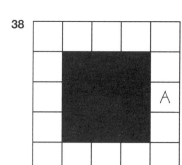

gravy, input, tangy, icing

39

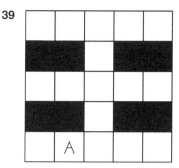

types, ultra, hasty, happy

40

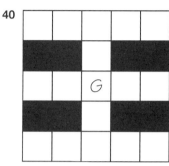

right, title, funny, night

5

Underline the one word in brackets which will go equally well with both pairs of words outside the brackets.

B 5

Example   rush, attack   cost, fee   (price, hasten, strike, <u>charge</u>, money)

41 kind, type   select, choose   (sort, gentle, take, pass, soft)

42 frolic, romp   performance, drama   (joy, act, jump, play, game)

43 insect, bug   travel, aeroplane   (fly, ant, hear, floor, listen)

44 attempt, try   knife, jab   (go, sword, stab, stake, point)

45 child, young   tease, fool   (kid, trick, badger, fox, tail)

5

46 If 7345 stands for TIME, 735 stands for _____ .

47 If 2839 stands for TAME, 382 stands for _____ .

48 If 4337 stands for DEER, 734 stands for _____ .

49 If 6913 stands for PEAL, 3916 stands for _____ .

50 If 4321 stands for LATE, 2341 stands for _____ .

B 24

5

In a class athletics competition, the blue team scored 20 points. The yellow team got five points more than the red team. The green team scored eight points less than the highest of these teams. The red team scored half as many points as the blue team.

B 25

51 Which team came top? _____

52 How many points did the yellow team score? _____

53 How many points did the red team score? _____

54 If it was Tuesday two days ago, what day will it be in five days' time? _____

55 If David will be 23 in four years' time, how old was he five years ago? _____

5

If a = 2, b = 4, c = 8, d = 6, e = 10 and f = 12, give the answers to these calculations as letters.

B 26

56 a + c = ____

57 f − c = ____

58 a × b = ____

59 a + b + d = ____

60 c ÷ a = ____

5

Answer these questions. The alphabet has been written out to help you.

B 20

A B C D E F G H I J K L M N O P Q R S T U V W X Y Z

61 Put the letters in MELTING in alphabetical order. _____

62 Which is now the last letter? _____

63 Which is now the second letter? _____

64 Put the letters in TRAYS in alphabetical order. _____

65 Which is now the third letter? _____

5

Now go to the Progress Chart to record your score!   Total   65

Paper 9

Find a word that is similar in meaning to the word in capital letters and that rhymes with the second word.

B 5

Example   CABLE   tyre   _wire_

1 LOAF   head   _____

2 CORRECT   flight   _____

3 BRAVE   hold   _____

4 SHOUT   dream   _____

5 SURPRISED   glazed   _____

5

Underline the one word in the brackets which is most opposite in meaning to the word in capitals.

B 6

Example   WIDE   (broad   vague   long   <u>narrow</u>   motorway)

6 JOYFUL   (old   rich   cheerful   sad   rested)

7 LOWER   (drop   raise   down   deep   below)

8 LEAVE   (behind   right   arrive   go   exit)

9 INCLUDE   (accept   exclude   add   remain   contain)

10 SEPARATE   (shrink   reduce   divide   apart   join)

5

Find the three-letter word which can be added to the letters in capitals to make a new word. The new word will complete the sentence sensibly.

B 22

Example   The cat sprang onto the MO.   <u>USE</u>

11 The musicians enjoyed playing their TPETS loudly.   _____

12 The food was very good at the Italian RESTAUT.   _____

13 The museum contained many royal CRS and robes.   _____

14 The choir was singing in perfect HONY.   _____

15 The swimming CHER asked the students to dive into the pool.   _____

5

Underline two words, one from each group, that go together to form a new word. The word in the first group always comes first.

B 8

Example   (hand, <u>green</u>, for)   (light, <u>house</u>, sure)

16 (under, side, on)   (take, put, out)

17 (to, where, up)   (good, right, may)

18 (at, through, in)   (out, last, fire)

19 (side, down, on)   (stairs, case, ladder)

20 (glass, drink, cup)   (board, set, light)

5

Find the four-letter word hidden at the end of one word and the beginning of the next word. The order of the letters may not be changed.

B 21

Example   The children had bats and balls.   <u>sand</u>

21 We will be the next group to get a table.   _____

22 Kate's rabbit enjoys munching on lettuce and carrots.   _____

23 Our holiday to Mauritius ended on a Saturday. _____

24 It is difficult to skip outside in the long grass. _____

25 My mum asked everyone to be quiet because the baby was sleeping. _____   ◯ 5

Move one letter from the first word and add it to the second word to make two new words.   B 13

    Example hunt sip   <u>hut</u> <u>snip</u>

26 flit   fame   _____ _____

27 sword   toll   _____ _____

28 smile   elf   _____ _____

29 fable   scar   _____ _____

30 robe   vent   _____ _____   ◯ 5

Complete the following sentences by selecting the most sensible word from each group of words given in the brackets. Underline the words selected.   B 14

    Example   The (<u>children</u>, books, foxes) carried the (houses, <u>books</u>, steps) home from the (greengrocer, <u>library</u>, factory).

31 The (score, goalkeeper, spectator) made a wonderful (save, fall, trick) to make sure we won the (treat, match, race).

32 (Eat, wash, dry) up your (water, vegetables, shoes) because they are (late, old, good) for you.

33 He was very (late, hungry, old) and found it hard to (dive, eat, walk) without a (dish, stick, paper).

34 Her (foot, dress, head) was very (modern, flat, wet) and had a wide (belt, eye, pot) on it.

35 Once upon a (day, year, time) in an (empty, ancient, easy) cottage there lived an old (witch, apple, child).   ◯ 5

Choose two words, one from each set of brackets, to complete the sentences in the best way.   B 15

    Example   Tall is to (tree, <u>short</u>, colour) as narrow is to (thin, white, <u>wide</u>).

36 Tiny is to (wild, small, huge) as long is to (last, little, short).

37 Late is to (first, early, behind) as calm is to (excited, easy, afraid).

38 Full is to (none, crowded, alone) as empty is to (bare, last, food).

39 Tie is to (shirt, bump, fasten) as turn is to (twist, knob, first).

40 Pause is to (continue, rest, worry) as remain is to (stay, important, leftover).   ◯ 5

Fill in the crosswords so that all the given words are included. You have been given one letter as a clue in each crossword.

41

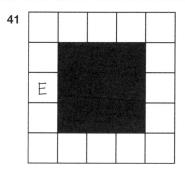

large, queer, range, quill

42

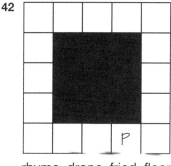

rhyme, drape, fried, floor

43

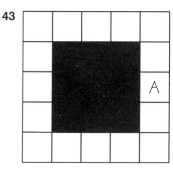

cheer, rifle, crepe, erase

44

fires, after, mitre, grave

45

thank, bites, taste, traps

Give the two missing pairs of letters and numbers in the following sequences. The alphabet has been written out to help you.

A B C D E F G H I J K L M N O P Q R S T U V W X Y Z

Example	CQ	DP	EQ	FP	_GQ_	_HP_
46	PC	PE	PG	PI	___	___
47	D	G	J	___	P	___
48	Y1	W3	U5	S7	___	___
49	CR	FP	IN	LL	___	___
50	AW	BV	DT	GQ	___	___

Here are the number codes for five words. Match the right word to the right code.

PAST	STAR	RATS	STIR	POST
5237	7325	1352	1852	5247

51 RATS   _____

52 STAR   _____

53 STIR   _____

54 PAST   _____

55 POST   _____

5

56 Arrange the letters in JACKPOTS in alphabetical order. _____

57 Which is now the last letter? _____

58 Which is now the fourth letter? _____

59 Arrange the letters in COUNTRY in alphabetical order. _____

60 Which is now the fifth letter? _____

5

Three little cats are called Jim, Jam and Jem. Jim is three years younger than Jam, but is two years older than Jem, who is five.

61 Who is the youngest? _____

62 How old is Jam? _____

2

Jean, Malek, Geeta, Martin and Sophie are students. Jean and Geeta speak English, German and Spanish. Sophie speaks Italian and German. Martin and Malek speak German, Italian and Spanish.

63 Which language is spoken by the fewest children? _____

64 Which language is spoken by the most children? _____

65 Which language is spoken by three children? _____

3

Paper 10

Underline the two words which are the odd ones out in the following groups of words.

Example black <u>king</u> purple green <u>house</u>

1 sponge   lake   ship   sea   ocean

2 crow   pigeon   twig   nest   eagle

3 love   heart   adore   friend   admire

4 next   aged   future   elderly   old

5 undecided   complicated   conclusion   termination   end

5

Find the three-letter word which can be added to the letters in capitals to make a new word. The new word will complete the sentence sensibly.

Example The cat sprang onto the MO. <u>USE</u>

6 Please DR up your juice.   _____

7 The meal lay half EA on the table.   _____

8 I think that you should COME the two options.   _____

9 Being POE is just good manners.   _____

10 I went to the paint shop with my Dad to decide which COL I wanted to paint my room.   _____

5

Underline the one word which **can be made** from the letters of the word in capital letters.

Example CHAMPION   camping notch peach cramp <u>chimp</u>

11 CONTROL   rot   cannot   call   roll   room

12 DECISION   slide   diesel   noisy   dice   scent

13 SLANDEROUS   gland   race   deal   slate   ended

14 INTOLERABLE   stale   strain   stable   bear   blame

15 ALLITERATION   creation   terrain   alight   terrapin   treat

5

Find the four-letter word hidden at the end of one word and the beginning of the next word. The order of the letters may not be changed.

Example The children had bats and balls. <u>sand</u>

16 Mum replied that Jake and Caleb aren't playing today.   _____

17 The zoo's alligator never came out of the pool except for food.   _____

18 In those days a serf earned his living with great difficulty.   _____

19 It is important to catch all shots coming in his direction.   _____

20 The star changed shape when looked at through the telescope.   _____

5

B 13

Move one letter from the first word and add it to the second word to make two new words.

    Example   hunt   sip   <u>hut</u>   <u>snip</u>

21 plate   cram   _____   _____

22 prime   gap   _____   _____

23 title   sigh   _____   _____

24 strand   bought   _____   _____

25 mince   lay   _____   _____

5

B 5

Find a word that is similar in meaning to the word in capital letters and that rhymes with the second word.

    Example   CABLE   tyre   <u>wire</u>

26 MEAL   crunch   _____

27 CRAFTY   fly   _____

28 STRIKE   clock   _____

29 JAB   croak   _____

30 COLOUR   bean   _____

5

B 14

Complete the following sentences by selecting the most sensible word from each group of words given in the brackets. Underline the words selected.

    Example   The (<u>children</u>, books, foxes) carried the (houses, <u>books</u>, steps) home from the (greengrocer, <u>library</u>, factory).

31 The (girl, ship, horse) was eating (water, hay, cable) in its (stable, current, bathroom).

32 Later that (week, day, night) an owl was heard (laughing, hooting, walking) in the (distance, flowers, table).

33 Before crossing the (river, road, sky) please look both (rafts, ways, eyes) and listen for (music, traffic, clouds).

34 The (manager, major, teacher) asked his (horses, customers, pupils) to hand in their (homework, teas, umbrellas).

35 The (girls, waiters, dentists) stood in line while their (mayor, mother, mechanic) bought tickets to the (cinema, wedding, party).

5

Find and underline the two words which need to change places for each sentence to make sense.

Example   She went to <u>letter</u> the <u>write</u>.

36 It was too outside to play rainy.

37 The last year of the day is a Sunday.

38 January is the month first of the year.

39 Did you have lunch for your lasagne?

40 The mother was crying until her baby gave her a dummy.

5

Fill in the missing letters and numbers. The alphabet has been written out to help you.

B 23

A B C D E F G H I J K L M N O P Q R S T U V W X Y Z

Example   AB is to CD as PQ is to R̲S̲.

41 TV is to SU as MO is to _____.

42 F6 is to H8 as Q17 is to _____.

43 AB is to EF as KL is to _____.

44 AC is to ZX as DF is to _____.

45 HJ is to QS as KM is to _____.

5

Underline the two words, one from each group, which are the most opposite in meaning.

B 9

Example   (dawn, <u>early</u>, wake) (<u>late</u>, stop, sunrise)

46 (quick, lazy, late)   (fast, slow, busy)

47 (change, hunt, save)   (spend, follow, lie)

48 (attempt, attack, attend)   (hold, try, retreat)

49 (far, near, away)   (distant, right, move)

50 (single, different, specific) (alone, general, unusual)

5

51–55 Write each word backwards and list them in alphabetical order.

B 20

retract   retreat   almost   enact   realistic

_____   _____   _____   _____   _____

5

If the code for STILE is 36192, what are the codes for the following words?

B 24

56 TIE   _____

57 LIES   _____

58 LIST   _____

3

39

If the code for RUSHES is 345725, what do the following codes stand for?

59 5432 _____

60 7425 _____

Ann likes sweets and toffee but not chocolate. Her sister, Jean, loves chocolate and fudge. Her friend Beata also likes chocolate and sweets, but hates fudge. Her sister Gosia likes chocolate and sweets.

61 Which two items are least popular? _____

62 Which two items are most popular? _____

Six children are lining up for the cinema. Mohammad is at the front and Ann is third in line. Eric does not stand next to Mohammad or Farook. Charlotte stands between Bob and Eric. Bob and Farook are not at the back of the line.

63 Who is last in line? _____

64 Who is between Farook and Bob? _____

65 Who is second in line? _____

Now go to the Progress Chart to record your score! **Total** 65

Paper 11

Underline the two words in each line which are most similar in type or meaning.

Example <u>dear</u>   pleasant   poor   extravagant   <u>expensive</u>

1 hungry   cheerful   sad   happy   wasteful

2 display   disappear   vanish   wonder   follow

3 flash   thunder   flare   burn   fall

4 sleep   eat   career   make   profession

5 pay   loss   deposit   consideration   salary

Find the three-letter word which can be added to the letters in capitals to make a new word. The new word will complete the sentence sensibly.

B 22

Example   The cat sprang onto the MO.   U_SE_

6 The lane was too NAR for a car.   _____

7 My favourite fruit is STBERRIES.   _____

8 A two-piece bathing suit is called a BII.   _____

9 Do not HEATE to call if you need further advice.   _____

10 I prefer NECINES to peaches.   _____

5

Find a word that can be put in front of each of the following words to make a new, compound word.

B 11

Example	cast	fall	ward	pour	_down_
11 work	boat	keeper	hold		_____
12 shell	shore	side	sick		_____
13 stairs	pour	hill	beat		_____
14 stage	bone	fire	stroke		_____
15 tower	dog	word	maker		_____

5

Find the four-letter word hidden at the end of one word and the beginning of the next word. The order of the letters may not be changed.

B 21

Example   The children had bats and balls.   _sand_

16 She somehow managed to lose her hat every week.   _____

17 The baby elephant sat down rather clumsily.   _____

18 We made the decorations ourselves.   _____

19 The tiny kittens lay peacefully on the rug.   _____

20 My dad complained because I left the fridge door open.   _____

5

Change the first word into the last word, by changing one letter at a time and making a new, different word in the middle.

B 11

Example   CASE   _CASH_   LASH

21 GALA   _____   GATE

22 PAST   _____   PORT

23 NEST   _____   BENT

24 CHEW   _____   BREW

25 STAR   _____   SPAT

5

Find and underline the two words which need to change places for each sentence to make sense.

Example   She went to <u>letter</u> the <u>write</u>.

26 The radio on the music was very relaxing.

27 We finally reach to managed the bus stop.

28 His birthday was on the last month of the day.

29 The old hunting were too tired to go lions.

30 Why are we having to queue in this long wait?

Fill in the crosswords so that all the given words are included. You have been given one letter as a clue in each crossword.

31

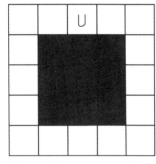

place, sleep, stunt, these

32

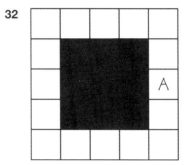

frown, names, slays, feels

33

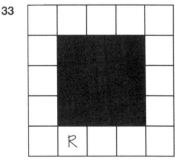

ended, freed, chose, chief

34

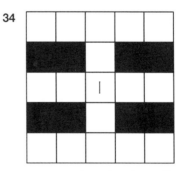

seven, prism, haste, veils

35

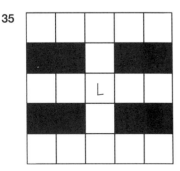

might, mists, poles, gales

Give the two missing pairs of letters in the following sequences. The alphabet has been written out to help you.

B 23

A B C D E F G H I J K L M N O P Q R S T U V W X Y Z

Example CQ DP EQ FP *GQ* *HP*

36 AC   AE   AG   AI   ___   ___

37 CG   FJ   IM   LP   ___   ___

38 DA   FC   HE   JG   ___   ___

39 BY   BW   CU   CS   ___   ___

40 MN   LO   KP   JQ   ___   ___

5

If the code for T E A C H E R is ▲ ♥ ◆ ○ • ♥ &. What are the codes for the following words?

B 24

41 ACHE   _____

42 REACH   _____

43 CHEAT   _____

What do these codes stand for?

44 • ♥ ◆ &   _____

45 & ◆ ▲ ♥   _____

5

46–47 Read the first statement and then underline two of the five options below that must be true.

B 25

'Eagles hunt small creatures for food.'

Eagles are wild.

Eagles eat mice.

Eagles cannot see well.

People hate eagles.

Eagles are predators.

2

48–49 Read the first two statements and then underline two of the five options below that must be true.

B 25

Palm trees only grow in hot countries. Palm trees are grown in Spain.

Spain is hot.

Palm trees are found in Ireland.

Palm trees never grow in cold countries.

Spain is a city.

Palm trees grow in Antarctica.

50–51 Read the first two statements and then underline two of the five options below that must be true. B 25

'Mercury and Venus are planets. They are closer to the Sun than Earth.'

Earth is hotter than Mars.

Earth is further from the Sun than Venus.

Mars is hotter than Venus.

Mercury and Earth are next to each other.

Venus is hotter than Earth.

2

Ewan, Joaquin, Alice and Gemma were discussing their favourite soap operas. Ewan and Alice are the only ones who like *Coronation Street*. Only Gemma and Alice like *Emmerdale*. Joaquin, Ewan and Gemma like *Eastenders*. B 25

52 Which is the most popular programme? _____

53 Who likes the fewest programmes? _____

2

Rashid, Peta, Molly, Annie and Tom were discussing whether they have a computer, a television or a stereo in their bedroom. Only Peta and Annie did not have a computer. Peta only had a television. Only Rashid and Tom did not have a television. Four children had a stereo. B 25

54 Who had a computer and television? _____

55 Who had all the same items? _____

2

If $p = 2$, $q = 4$, $r = 6$, $s = 8$, $t = 10$ and $u = 12$, give the answer to these calculations as letters. B 26

56 $q + r =$ _____

57 $u - s =$ _____

58 $p \times q =$ _____

59 $u \div p =$ _____

60 $p \times (u - r) =$ _____

5

Solve the problems by working out the letter codes. The alphabet has been written out to help you. B 24

A B C D E F G H I J K L M N O P Q R S T U V W X Y Z

61 In a code, FINAL is written as HKPCN. What is the code for NAIL? _____

62 In a code, BROWN is written as AQNVM. How would you write REST? _____

63 In a code, MILK is written as NJML. What does HPPE stand for? _____

64 In a code, BACK is written as ABBL. How would you write CRY? _____

65 In a code, PRESS is written as MOBPP. How would you write TOUGH? _____

5

Paper 12

Underline the two words which are the odd ones out in the following groups of words.

    Example   black   <u>king</u>   purple   green   <u>house</u>

1 long   wide   smart   short   fast

2 head   ankle   body   leg   smile

3 oak   mud   sand   beech   elm

4 river   desert   stream   brook   ocean

5 catch   field   haul   meadow   drag

Find the three-letter word which can be added to the letters in capitals to make a new word. The new word will complete the sentence sensibly.

    Example   The cat sprang onto the MO.   <u>USE</u>

6 Please SHAR your pencil.   ———————

7 The lack of rain has caused a HOSEE ban.   ———————

8 We do ITION and subtraction in maths.   ———————

9 I had to SCH my room this morning when I couldn't find my homework.   ———————

10 The teacher asked the pupils to take out some PR and a pen.   ———————

Find the letter which will complete both pairs of words, ending the first word and starting the second. The same letter must be used for both pairs of words.

    Example   mea (<u>t</u>) able   fi (<u>t</u>) ub

11 ever (—) ellow   happ (—) ule

12 faste (—) uby   mise (—) oute

13 frigh (—) error   spa (—) able

14 rea (—) ise   pai (—) ound

15 fou (—) ight   cal (—) oad

Underline two words, one from each group, that go together to form a new word. The word in the first group always comes first.

    Example   (hand, <u>green</u>, for)   (light, <u>house</u>, sure)

16 (net, side, hat)   (ball, case, mug)

17 (flat, hard, big)   (room, age, mate)

18 (hit, tap, pat)   (ten, tear, tern)

19 (poor, open, good)   (can, door, will)

20 (car, fan, man)   (ate, ear, age)

Find the four-letter word hidden at the end of one word and the beginning of the next word. The order of the letters may not be changed.

> **Example**   The children had bats and balls.   <u>sand</u>

21 The king finished his speech by wishing everyone goodnight.   _____

22 The old man enjoyed seeing his grandchildren.   _____

23 The Pope arrived back at the Vatican late that night.   _____

24 They sat under the umbrella and talked until the sun went down.   _____

25 Clodagh was very brave in the hospital.   _____

Move one letter from the first word and add it to the second word to make two new words.

> **Example**   hunt   sip   <u>hut</u>   <u>snip</u>

26 shelf   sell   _____   _____

27 brown   shoe   _____   _____

28 share   mash   _____   _____

29 crate   pat   _____   _____

30 least   ton   _____   _____

Find and underline the two words which need to change places for each sentence to make sense.

> **Example**   She went to <u>letter</u> the <u>write</u>.

31 When the wind blows the trees fall from the leaves.

32 He thought that he had come race in the first.

33 Please eat your bowl and clear away your breakfast.

34 The winner won a silver medal and the runner-up a gold one.

35 You have to find deep to dig the hidden treasure.

Fill in the missing letters. The alphabet has been written out to help you.

A B C D E F G H I J K L M N O P Q R S T U V W X Y Z

Example   AB is to CD as PQ is to R̲S̲.

36 BR is to DT as FV is to _____.

37 XU is to UR as TQ is to _____.

38 PN is to TJ is to SQ is to _____.

39 WA is to WB is to WC is to _____.

40 MN is to LO as KP is to _____.

Here are the number codes for five words. Match the right word to the right code.

PART	PANE	NEAR	PINE	NINE
2849	2528	3528	3491	3428

41 PART   _____

42 PANE   _____

43 PINE   _____

44 NEAR   _____

45 NINE   _____

Five children: Danny, Ella, Petra, Li and Sharif have pets. Petra has a goldfish and a hamster. Ella, Danny and Li have cats. Sharif, Li, Danny and Ella have dogs. Li does not like hamsters, but has a mouse.

46 Who has the most pets?   _____

47 Which pets does Danny have?   _____

48 Who only has a dog?   _____

49 In five years' time Annabelle will be 10.
     How old was she three years ago?   _____

50   In two years' time Jamie will be half the age of his sister,
      who is 12 now. How old is Jamie now?   _____

If D = 2, F = 4, H = 6, J = 12, and L = 24, give the answers to these calculations as letters.

51 D + D + D = _____

52 J – H = _____

53 D × D = _____

54 L ÷ J = _____

55   D × (H ÷ D) = _____

B 23

5

B 24

5

B 25

3

B 25

2

B 26

5

Change one word so that the sentence makes sense. Underline the word you are taking out and write your new word on the line.

Example   I waited in line to buy a <u>book</u> to see the film.   *ticket*

56 I went to the flower station to fill up my car for the long journey.   _____

57 Ellen took her sick hamster to the garage.   _____

58 The cat liked to sleep near the window to catch the
last of the moon's rays.   _____

59 The swan stretched its graceful, long foot as it floated in the pond.   _____

60 My favourite sort of ice marshmallow is chocolate.   _____

5

Solve the problems by working out the letter codes. The alphabet has been written out to help you.

A B C D E F G H I J K L M N O P Q R S T U V W X Y Z

61 In a code, FASTER is written as IDVWHU. How would you write RATES?_____

62 In a code, SPORT is written as URQTV. How would you write PLUM?   _____

63 In a code, MOST is written as NQVX. What does TCOI stand for?   _____

64 In a code, BEAN is written as DCCL. What does UFQU stand for?   _____

65 In a code, CREST is written as FUHVW. How would you write MASK?   _____

5

Now go to the Progress Chart to record your score!   **Total**   65

Paper 13

Look at these groups of words.

A	B	C	D
beef	orange	water	potato
lamb	pear	lemonade	cabbage
pork	cherry	coffee	pea

Choose the correct group for each of the words below. Write in the letter.

1 lemon   _____

2 spinach   _____

3 tea   _____

4 chicken   _____

5 grape   _____

5

Underline the two words, one from each group, which are closest in meaning.

Example (race, shop, start)   (finish, begin, end)

6 (old, patterned, hunt)   (new, search, faint)

7 (similar, opposite, wide)   (afar, last, alike)

8 (out, back, overtake)   (pass, front, in)

9 (show, contain, hide)   (display, cry, guess)

10 (clean, tidy, vague)   (sunny, explained, unclear)

B 3

5

Underline one word in the brackets which is most opposite in meaning to the word in capitals.

B 6

Example WIDE   (broad vague long narrow motorway)

11 FAIL   (work point pass fade call)

12 PEACE   (quiet softness old calm conflict)

13 REPAIR   (fix push damage flatten paint)

14 LEAD   (chase trail pant follow hound)

15 CERTAIN   (sure absolute positive true doubtful)

5

Underline the one word in the brackets which will go equally well with both the pairs of words outside the brackets.

B 5

Example rush, attack   cost, fee   (price, hasten, strike, charge, money)

16 pot, tin   able, willing   (box, well, metal, can, agreeable)

17 delicate, weightless   ignite, flare   (light, heavy, hot, dim, flat)

18 smack, strike   success, chart-topper   (pat, stroke, winning, hit, put)

19 light, shining   able, clever   (fired, ablaze, bright, cunning, lively)

20 elegant, stylish   hurt, ache   (neat, painful, tidy, paranoid, smart)

5

Find a word that can be put in front of each of the following words to make new, compound words.

B 11

Example cast   fall   ward   pour   _down_

21 house   fly   grocer   finch   _____

22 pecker   worm   cutter   wind   _____

23 place   arm   fighter   side   _____

24 bag   shake   rail   writing   _____

25 brush   cut   band   dresser   _____

5

Find the four-letter word hidden at the end of one word and the beginning of the next word. The order of the letters may not be changed.

Example The children had bats and balls. _sand_

26 All the boys and girls played sensibly at break-time. _____

27 Alex was ready for his grand gala centenary celebrations. _____

28 The famous actor never once forgot her lines. _____

29 After my hard work, I was glad to have scored top in my class. _____

30 I usually read for thirty minutes before I go to bed. _____

Remove one letter from the word in capital letters to leave a new word. The meaning of the new word is given in the clue.

Example AUNT an insect _ant_

31 MEAN male _____

32 STORE painful _____

33 PILOT plan _____

34 SHOP jump _____

35 TRIP tear _____

Find and underline the two words which need to change places for each sentence to make sense.

Example She went to <u>letter</u> the <u>write</u>.

36 We put the cake in the bake to oven.

37 We put the names in alphabetical order so Bindy came before Annabel.

38 I sometimes count on my homework when doing my maths fingers.

39 The red rose is often white or wild in colour.

40 I have red seven pages in my read level book.

Find the letter which will end the first word and start the second word.

Example peac (<u>h</u>) ome

41 star (___) arth

42 cras (___) all

43 hai (___) ail

44 pac (___) ear

45 el (___) new

Here are the number codes for five words. Match the right word to the right code.

BOOT	FALL	ALTO	TOOL	BAIL
3297	5117	3115	8277	2751

46 BOOT   ———

47 FALL   ———

48 ALTO   ———

49 TOOL   ———

50 BAIL   ———

5

Peter, David and Asif sit in a row in class. David is not beside Asif, who sits on the right of the three.

51 Who sits on the left?   ————————

52 Who is in the middle?   ————————

2

53 In six years' time Alice will be twice as old as her sister,
who is two now. How old will Alice be?   ————

54 Four years ago Robert was five. In five years' time he
will be half the age of his brother. How old is his brother now?   ————

55 Town A is south of town B, east of town D and west of town F.
Town C is north-east of town A. Which town is furthest west?   ————

3

Rearrange the letters in capitals to make another word. The new word has something to do with the first two words.

Example spot soil SAINT <u>STAIN</u>

56 twos   doubles   PARIS   ————

57 goes out   leaves   EXIST   ————

58 dressing   gravy   CAUSE   ————

59 herb   wise   AGES   ————

60 hazard   risk   GARDEN   ————

5

Change one word so that the sentence makes sense. Underline the word you are taking out and write your new word on the line.

B 14

Example   I waited in line to buy a <u>book</u> to see the film.   *ticket*

61 The butcher had baked several cakes.   _____

62 Tame animals do not make very good pets.   _____

63 The bird had constructed a beautiful hole out of twigs.   _____

64 Sunday is the last month of the calendar year.   _____

65 The nurse asked her pupils to take their seats.   _____   **5**

Now go to the Progress Chart to record your score!   **Total   65**

Paper 14

Underline the pair of words most similar in meaning.

B 5

Example   come, go   <u>roam, wander</u>   fear, fare

1 hurry, rest   swift, fast   break, fix

2 back, rear   hold, tie   under, over

3 polish, dirty   hunt, dog   miniature, small

4 shoot, score   aim, goal   wind, wave

5 take, give   prize, present   pole, rod   **5**

Underline the pair of words most opposite in meaning.

B 9

Example   cup, mug   coffee, milk   <u>hot, cold</u>

6 wide, open   brilliant, dull   over, beyond

7 start, begin   fade, flatten   rude, polite

8 rise, fall   flake, drop   bounce, jump

9 post, join   criticise, praise   cry, wail

10 relaxed, tense   teach, instruct   lose, misplace   **5**

Underline the one word in the brackets which will go equally well with both the pairs of words outside the brackets.

Example   rush, attack   cost, fee   (price, hasten, strike, <u>charge</u>, money)

11 obvious, apparent   fields, grassland   (clear, plain, lawn, simple, ordinary)

12 elegance, beauty   prayer, thanks   (grace, amen, goodwill, attraction, power)

13 fill, arrange   bundle, parcel   (swell, gift, pack, place, pile)

14 particle, speck   cereal, seed   (piece, corn, bit, plant, grain)

15 sun, sky   celebrity, actor   (moon, star, shine, head, main)

Find the letter which will complete both pairs of words, ending the first word and starting the second. The same letter must be used for both pairs of words.

Example   mea ($\underline{t}$) able   fi ($\underline{t}$) ub

16 star (——) ver   man (——) ntry

17 car   (——) angy   hin (——) umble

18 sa   (——) ame   ho   (——) rink

19 plan (——) ill   hun (——) nit

20 sou (——) ale   ram (——) rove

Find the four-letter word hidden at the end of one word and the beginning of the next word. The order of the letters may not be changed.

Example   The children had bats and balls.   <u>sand</u>

21 Who let the cat in?   ——————

22 My dad's shed generally is rather messy.   ——————

23 Tremors from a severe earthquake can end up many miles away.   ——————

24 Fraser lent Sam a pencil because he'd left his at home.   ——————

25 I understand that aspirin deadens pain in the back.   ——————

Change the first word into the last word, by changing one letter at a time and making a new, different word in the middle.

Example   CASE   <u>CASH</u>   LASH

26 PANT   ——————   PARK

27 MOST   ——————   MINT

28 SOUR   ——————   SEAR

29 BEAT   ——————   BRAG

30 NUTS   ——————   CATS

Look at the first group of three words. The word in the middle has been made from the other two words. Complete the second group of three words in the same way, making a new word in the middle of the group.

Example PAIN INTO TOOK   ALSO <u>SOON</u> ONLY

31	PALE	PEST	STIR	TAKE	_____	STOP
32	SOAR	OAST	TIME	SALE	_____	ONLY
33	FOOL	LOST	MAST	LEAP	_____	STAR
34	PRICE	RACE	PANIC	SPELT	_____	BISON
35	STEAM	LATE	CLEAR	TREND	_____	CREAM

Find the letter which will end the first word and start the second word.

Example peac (<u>h</u>) ome

36 caree (___) ent

37 fir (___) dge

38 car (___) here

39 fee (___) rack

40 lam (___) arrel

Underline the two words, one from each group, which are closest in meaning.

Example (race, shop, <u>start</u>)   (finish, <u>begin</u>, end)

41 (pound, paint, wash)   (beat, drop, destroy)

42 (lower, move, turn)   (raise, reduce, tear)

43 (mould, attach, injure)   (damage, remove, subtract)

44 (game, sickness, pattern)   (repair, chess, illness)

45 (knotty, spoilt, tough)   (weak, blessed, strong)

Find a word that can be put in front of each of the following words to make a new, compound word.

Example cast   fall   ward   pour   *down*

46	lock	fare	lord	path	_____
47	fowl	front	logged	course	_____
48	proof	board	man	vane	_____
49	over	book	port	word	_____
50	ache	space	ground	pack	_____

Give the two missing pairs of letters and numbers. The alphabet has been written out to help you.

B 23

A B C D E F G H I J K L M N O P Q R S T U V W X Y Z

Example   CQ   DP   EQ   FP   _GQ_   _HP_

51   AL   EL   IM   MM   ___   ___

52   AA   ZZ   BB   YY   ___   ___

53   ZX   XV   VT   TR   ___   ___

54   NM   NO   ON   OP   ___   ___

55   A1   C2   E3   G4   ___   ___

5

If ← ↑ → ↓ ↔ ϒ ↑ is the code for REPLACE, what do these codes stand for?

B 24

56   → ↑ ↔ ←   _____

57   ϒ ↓ ↔ →   _____

58   → ↔ ↓ ↑   _____

59   ↓ ↑ ↑ ←   _____

60   → ↔ ↓ ↔ ϒ ↑   _____

5

Change one word so that the sentence makes sense. Underline the word you are taking out and write your new word on the line.

B 14

Example   I waited in line to buy a <u>book</u> to see the film.   _ticket_

61   Mrs Stokes found that a glass of warm milk helped her wake at night.   _____

62   One of Roger's guitar notes broke as he practised.   _____

63   After being fatally wounded, the soldier was pronounced alive when he reached the hospital.   _____

64   Watching the moon rise is a wonderful way to start the morning.   _____

65   I was so hungry because I ate all of my dinner and then had a second helping.   _____

5

Now go to the Progress Chart to record your score!   Total   65

Paper 15

Underline the two words, one from each group, which are closest in meaning.

B 3

Example   (race, shop, <u>start</u>)   (finish, <u>begin</u>, end)

1   (speak, take, ask)   (request, put, give)

2   (rough, shiny, clean)   (wild, glistening, dirty)

3 (destroyed, repaired, reformed)   (closed, compared, broken)

4 (cross, flighty, upset)   (angry, cheerful, pale)

5 (drum, stick, noise)   (tap, loud, music)

B 9

Underline the two words, one from each group, which are the most opposite in meaning.

    Example (dawn, <u>early</u>, wake)   (<u>late</u>, stop, sunrise)

6 (shy, old, late)   (aged, confident, true)

7 (cause, result, outcome)   (effect, mistake, hide)

8 (follow, collect, light)   (win, heavy, succeed)

9 (tired, controlled, hungry)   (starving, thirsty, energetic)

10 (numb, hurting, rare)   (painful, common, protected)

Find the letter which will end the first word and start the second word.

B 10

    Example peac (<u>h</u>) ome

11 pai (___) ule

12 fi (___) ase

13 too (___) ast

14 cove (___) ain

15 pun (___) oung

Find the four-letter word hidden at the end of one word and the beginning of the next word. The order of the letters may not be changed.

B 21

    Example The children had bats and balls.   <u>sand</u>

16 You are lucky as it is the final one in the shop.   _____

17 He considered the cash unnecessary in the circumstances.   _____

18 The Incas taught us many interesting things.   _____

19 The crowd quit cheering when the team lost the ball.   _____

20 He ate the bag of sweets himself.   _____

Which one letter can be added to the front of all these words to make new words?

B 12

    Example <u>c</u>are   <u>c</u>at   <u>c</u>rate   <u>c</u>all

21 ___reak   ___rand   ___all   ___oat

22 ___oat   ___ool   ___lean   ___hain

23	___ake	___orn	___oad	___urn
24	___ir	___ate	___ind	___ault
25	___ind	___est	___ould	___hite

5

Remove one letter from the word in capital letters to leave a new word. The meaning of the new word is given in the clue.

B 12

Example AUNT   an insect   ant

26 DRAGOON   mythical beast   _____

27 COVER   bay   _____

28 ORATION   limited amount   _____

29 SHINE   leg   _____

30 METEOR   measuring instrument   _____

5

Find and underline the two words which need to change places for each sentence to make sense.

B 17

Example She went to <u>letter</u> the <u>write</u>.

31 The old track chugged along the endless train.

32 England is one of the largest counties in Kent.

33 I really enjoy classical films and black and white music.

34 It was very home so I ran briskly late.

35 The house was delivered to the wrong newspaper by mistake.

5

Choose two words, one from each set of brackets, to complete the sentences in the best way.

B 15

Example Tall is to (tree, <u>short</u>, colour) as narrow is to (thin, white, <u>wide</u>).

36 Speedy is to (fast, slow, late) as low is to (last, high, calm).

37 Ignore is to (overlook, welcome, accept) as praise is to (forget, change, honour).

38 Well is to (water, ill, better) as mine is to (wood, coal, wheat).

39 Damp is to (wet, sandy, dry) as cool is to (snow, rain, cold).

40 Kite is to (fly, sky, bird) as badger is to (nest, zoo, mammal).

5

If A = 1, B = 4, D = 5, E = 10, S = 20, what are the sums of the following words by adding the letters together?

41 BAD = _____

42 SEED = _____

Give the answer to these calculations as letters.

43 S – E = _____

44 (A + B) + D = _____

45 E – D = _____

B 26

5

Find the letter which will complete both pairs of words, ending the first word and starting the second. The same letter must be used for both pairs of words.

Example   mea (t) able   fi (t) ub

46 clai (___) ost   cal (___) en

47 pra (___) olk   tr (___) oung

48 pac (___) nd   craz (___) ase

49 bal (___) ose   foo (___) eck

50 ful (___) oot   scraw (___) and

B 10

5

Rearrange the letters in capitals to make another word. The new word has something to do with the first two words.

Example   spot   soil   SAINT   STAIN

51 jump   hop   PALE   _____

52 untrue   unreal   FLEAS   _____

53 not strong   fragile   WAKE   _____

54 annoys   upsets   RANGES   _____

55 fruit   canteloupe   LEMON   _____

B 16

5

Change the first word into the last word, by changing one letter at a time and making a new, different word in the middle.

Example   CASE   CASH   LASH

56 POST   _____   PACT

57 MICE   _____   MATE

58 ARTS   _____   AIMS

59 SHIP   _____   SNAP

60 FLOW   _____   FLAT

B 13

5

Fill in the missing letters and numbers. The alphabet has been written out to help you.

A B C D E F G H I J K L M N O P Q R S T U V W X Y Z

Example   AB is to CD as PQ is to R̲S̲.

61 DN is to BL as GQ is to _____.

62 BB is to YY as DD is to _____.

63 JJ is to LM as QQ is to _____.

64 ZY is to ZX as ZW is to _____.

65 A1 is to D2 as Y25 is to _____.

5

Now go to the Progress Chart to record your score!   Total   65

Progress Chart Verbal Reasoning 9–10 years Book 2

Total marks ▼

Paper ▼

Percentage ▼

Total marks	Paper 1	2	3	4	5	6	7	8	9	10	11	12	13	14	15	Percentage
65																100%
60																90%
55																85%
																80%
50																
45																70%
40																60%
35																50%
30																
25																40%
20																30%
15																20%
10																
5																10%
0	1	2	3	4	5	6	7	8	9	10	11	12	13	14	15	0%

Date ▶

When you've finished the book use the Next Steps Planner ▶